Brown
Bomber

Brown Bomber

Barney Nagler

WORLD PUBLISHING
TIMES MIRROR
NEW YORK

PHOTO CREDITS

Page 9 (of photo insert), bottom right, United Press
International; page 13, top, United Press International; page 15, bottom, Wide World Photos; page
16, top, Wide World Photos; page 16, bottom,
United Press International; all other photos courtesy
of *The Ring* magazine.

Published by The World Publishing Company
Published simultaneously in Canada
by Nelson, Foster & Scott Ltd.
First printing—1972
Copyright © 1972 by Barney Nagler
All rights reserved
ISBN 0-529-04522-2
Library of Congress catalog card number: 71-183089
Printed in the United States of America
Designed by Jacques Chazaud

WORLD PUBLISHING
TIMES MIRROR

1

It was just before four o'clock that Friday afternoon in May when the sheriff's deputies reached Joe Louis's house, though he would not know until later that they were there. He was, as usual, looking at television, biting into an apple, apparently at peace with himself. The days were not his enemies. He lived the nights in a sullen dream blighted by an inward remorse, fearing ambassadors of hate who never arrived. A shadow had come over him, growing thicker and darker in the privacy of his mind, and only daylight brought release.

He had been the heavyweight champion of the world, and people had come to adore him. Those who had ob-

[1]

served him at close range were impressed by his willingness, even eagerness, to make frank assessments of his
liabilities. Whatever his faults, and they were many, he
often faced the truth and laughed at himself. He had
squandered millions, but this had not diminished his
laughter. When, finally, he owed $1,250,000 in income
taxes and penalties, the government gave up on him, even
while keeping his name on the roll of tax debtors. Only
when his mind betrayed him was there a change. And
now, within a fortnight of his fifty-sixth birthday, the
world was about to close in on him.

For several years Louis had resisted the recommendation of physicians that he was in need of psychiatric
treatment. He believed that members of the Mafia were
pursuing him, intent on destroying him with poison gas.
Wherever he went, he perceived them in his conscious-
ness, and they provoked outbursts of suspicion and rage.

Formerly he had worked out his inner hostilities in
the ring. Outside the ring, he consumed himself in frivolity
and made many mistakes, none of which he blamed on
others. Despite his affection for the sweeter life, he had
always displayed a certain disgust for hypocrisy, restric-
tions, and self-deception. When, finally, he was overcome
by bizarre aberrations, he was suddenly devoid of dignity,
pride, and determination. He externalized his fantasies,
and this rendered him a pitiable figure.

Just a few days before that fateful Friday he had
returned to his home in Denver with his wife Martha.
Arriving there, he went to his bedroom and tried to sleep.
As he had been doing lately, he slept with his clothes on,
wary of imagined intruders.

In the morning, Mrs. Louis went into her husband's bedroom. He was awake, sitting slope-shouldered on the edge of the bed, his eyes narrow and resentful.

"See," he said, with tired anger in his voice, "your friends bugged the house. I found it."

Martha Louis inspected the lamp on the table near the bed. Her husband had torn it apart, disclosing its harmless internal wiring.

"What do you mean, my friends?" she snapped. "You weren't coming here when we left Los Angeles. You were going to Washington to play in a golf tournament. Nobody knew you were coming to Denver."

He went quiet, the anger going out of him, and he was abruptly docile.

Mrs. Louis, the third wife of the former prizefighter, is in her fifties, a wiry, resourceful woman with high cheekbones and a quickness of eye that suggests an alertness of mind. Until the advent of Louis's mental illness, she had been a successful trial lawyer in Los Angeles. But Louis's condition had altered her circumstances and she was, in the spring of 1970, devoting most of her time to her husband.

In conformity with Colorado law, she acted to have her husband committed to a psychiatric hospital for examination and treatment. She had moved quietly to accomplish this purpose, not that the truth of Louis's mental illness was in the least secret. His friends knew of his misery, but they maintained a discreet silence in public. Only when they were alone with him did they talk about it, and even then they tried to pass it off by laughing at his affliction, which they regarded lightly.

[3]

No laughter in this regard sounded in the throats of Louis's two children by his first wife. Both his son and daughter had concurred in their stepmother's decision to submit their father to institutionalized psychiatric examination.

Joseph Louis Barrow, Jr.—he uses his father's real surname—was twenty-three years of age and a junior executive in the trust department of the United Bank of Denver. At night he studied law at the University of Denver, where he had received a bachelor of arts degree in political science. His sister, Jacqueline, was twenty-seven years of age and a former student at Fisk University. She had been married and divorced. Because she preferred the climate of California, she lived with her father and stepmother in their apartment in Los Angeles.

Late in April, Mrs. Louis had prevailed upon her husband to accompany her to Denver. She liked Denver, but he could take it or leave it. Some years before she had bought the house at 2675 Monaco Parkway for $30,000. When Louis learned that she was negotiating for the purchase of the brick ranch house, he asked, "Where's the golf course?"

"A few blocks away," she said, "down Twenty-sixth Street across Colorado Boulevard."

"Buy it," he said.

Despite its proximity to the golf course, where he could pursue his favorite pastime, he came to dislike the house. Las Vegas or New York was his alternate world. In Las Vegas he found excitement at the tables. He was a hapless gambler and usually lost, but it did not matter because the money he lost was provided by the hotel management, first at the Thunderbird and more recently at Caesars Palace. It was good business to have him around. He was permitted to keep his winnings; but luck did not often reward him, and the money stayed with the establishment.

When he was in New York, he ran around with old boxing friends. He felt free and could do as he pleased, holed up at the Park Sheraton Hotel, spending many days in bed watching television, a mesmeric way of making time pass. But what he wanted mostly was fun.

Women found him sexually appealing, and he was activated by their physical presence. Around them, he laughed easily. His relationship with them was a game he played. Martha Louis insisted that her husband was a submissive victim of the need for competition. She once told him, "Joe, I don't think any woman affects you. I think sex to you is something apart, just as methodical as going into the ring and knocking somebody out."

"You a funny woman," he replied. He respected her perception.

Now, on that day in May in Denver, she was concerned only with her husband's apparently inexplicable mental disorder. It was not a matter of chance that he was in Denver with her. She had planned it that way. And when the sheriff's deputies came to take Joe Louis away, she was not even at home.

2

Mrs. Martha Malone Jefferson had never known a
prizefighter before she met Joe Louis in 1957. A
mutual friend introduced them, and they chatted on the
telephone even before they saw each other. Then, some
weeks after their first conversation, Louis phoned Mrs.
Jefferson and said he would like to visit her in Los Angeles. When friends first saw them together, they asked
her, "How in hell did you ever meet him?" to which she
replied, "How in hell did he ever meet me?"

Though not as well known as Louis, who was a
source of black pride everywhere, her name was respect-
fully recognized in legal circles and in the Negro community of Los Angeles. For seven years she had been married

to Bernard Jefferson, with whom she shared a law practice, but there had been a divorce before she met Louis. Even after the divorce, she continued her partnership with her former husband, who later became a Superior Court judge in Los Angeles.

Always certain of what she wanted from the world, she had gone from her home in Palestine, Texas, to Tuskegee Institute in Alabama, and, later, to Southwestern Law School in Los Angeles. Her parents were disappointed when she chose Tuskegee. They were pious Baptists and had expected her to enroll in Bishop College, a Baptist school in Dallas. "I don't want a denominational school," she told them. "Booker T. Washington was a poor man when he founded Tuskegee. I want to be a poor girl in a poor man's school." By the time she met Louis, she had been a member of the California bar for fourteen years and was prosperous.

Their first meeting was on March 11, 1957. She drove out to International Airport to meet Louis's plane from Chicago, where he was living at the time. She liked Louis immediately and considered him, for a man of his background, gentlemanly and amusing. It was a genial event, and she was pleased to be in his company. She had, of course, known about him. Everything she had read about him made her believe, in her phrase, that he wouldn't dirty two bedsheets if he got between them.

Louis was still married to his second wife, Rose Morgan, though he no longer was living with her. She ran a cosmetics business in Harlem. When they separated, he moved to Chicago. The separation had been friendly, and later Rose Morgan laughingly remembered that one of the major problems in their marriage was Louis's sleeping habits. He would stay in bed all day and stay out all night. When his wife scolded him and told him this could not go on, he told her not to worry: he would wait until she fell asleep before going out. The way it turned out, she would stay awake until 3:00 A.M.—and he would fall asleep.

Louis and Rose Morgan had announced their plan to be married while visiting Louis's former manager, Marshall Miles, in Buffalo. Miles told Joe, "You're making a mistake. You're both nice people, but you're not for each other." And he told Miss Morgan, "Joe's broke, you know. He doesn't have a penny." But on Christmas Day, 1955, Louis married Rose Morgan. Two years later they separated; and when the marriage was annulled, they were still good friends.

In regard to Louis's marital status, Martha Jefferson had no qualms. She was not thinking of marriage when she met Louis, and by the time they were married, on March 11, 1959, Rose Morgan had gone her own way in New York. On the morning of the wedding, the bride fussed with her hair in her Los Angeles home and then, accompanied by Louis, drove her Cadillac to the little California town of Winter Haven, near the Arizona border, where they were married by a justice of the peace. A week later the news leaked out. Unlike Louis's first marriage, it did not make newspaper headlines.

When Louis married Marva Trotter, he was twenty-one years of age and at the top of his bent as a fighter. He was known as the "Brown Bomber," a powerful puncher up from a sharecropper's cotton patch in Alabama, suddenly rich from the proceeds of his ring labors, and he was a black hero. In twenty-four successful fights, he had knocked out twenty opponents, and there was every indication that he would become the heavyweight champion of the world. But even then the realities of his life did not conform to the image imposed on him by sportswriters. They had written, in the rhetoric of their time, that he was a natural killer and attributed to him no romantic counterpoint. He had fooled them. He had fallen in love.

In the winter of 1934, toward the end of Louis's first year as a professional fighter, he met Marva Trotter. A friend, Gerard Hughes, brought her to Trafton's Gymnasium in Chicago, where Louis was in training. The young boxer took one look at Marva and she became important to him. Her mocha chocolate skin was smooth, and she wore her hair drawn back tightly, revealing a high forehead. Her dark eyes were bright and beguiling, complementing her fine nose and wide mouth. Her garb, moderate in color and style, swaddled a curvaceous figure. She danced well and spoke easily, and most of all she knew how to laugh at Louis's jokes. His humor was broad, and when she laughed, she made him glow all over. But he was mostly silent during their courtship and, she remembers, "romantic in a quiet sort of way." His free-wheeling attitude toward women had not yet developed. Ten months after he met her, Louis married Marva Trotter.

Louis's life was like a kite nobody could reel in. People followed him everywhere, reaching to touch him, clamoring for his autograph. Not even their private wedding could be hidden from public view. It took place a few hours before Louis was to go up to Yankee Stadium to fight Max Baer, a former heavyweight champion. Marva's brother, the Reverend Walter Trotter, had come from

Chicago to perform the ceremony in the Harlem apartment of a friend, Lucille Armstead. When Louis tried to reach the apartment, the halls were so crowded with well-wishers, newspaper reporters, and photographers, he had to climb down a fire escape to avoid the crush. Later, Marva went to the stadium to see her husband knock out Baer within four rounds.

There was no honeymoon trip. Instead, the couple returned to Chicago, where 10,000 persons stood in the street in front of the South Side apartment house in which they were to live, and cheered them. They went out on a porch and waved to the crowd. Then Louis threw his hat into the crowd, and there was a rush to capture it as a good-luck token. The newlyweds went back into their apartment. Outside, the crowd drifted away.

Louis was still the world heavyweight champion when his son was born on May 28, 1947. The infant resembled his father. "He's built like me, only vest-size," Louis said, so they called the baby "Punchy." Before Joseph Louis Barrow, Jr., was two years old, his parents were no longer together. They had first been divorced in March 1945 and had remarried in Mexico a short time later. The second marriage was of brief duration. A divorce, obtained by Marva Louis in Jojutla in the Mexican state of Morelos in February 1949, provided for Louis to pay $100 weekly in support of Punchy, who would join his sister, Jacqueline, in the custody of their mother.

When he was growing up, Punchy did not see much of his father. He felt, he said later, "distant from him," explaining, "When I was a kid, maybe four years old, I didn't have any conception of how famous he was. I just knew he was a famous man, a prizefighter. He would come to our house sporadically and he would take us out to dinner, or something. I remember riding through Washington Park in Chicago once and just asking him a question: 'Is this going to be your last fight?' He said 'Yeah.' He must have been talking about the fight with Rocky Marciano. I recall being very sad that he had to do it again."

And that, really, was all of the son's early recollection of his father. People asked him, "You going to be a fighter?" And he would reply, "One champion in the family is enough." Small and mostly placid, he had no instinct for fighting. His mother had married Dr. Albert Lee Spaulding, a physician, and their home at Forty-eighth and Woodlawn in the Hyde Park section of Chicago was filled with talk of everything but boxing. In this environment, his mind automatically rejected the violence of the ring.

He was seventeen years of age and a student at Boston University when he decided that he ought to get closer to his father. He thought, "It would be a shame to have a father like him and not really know him." When he was on vacation, he arranged to meet Louis on weekends. Their meetings were strained. "He's friendly and warm, as warm as he can be," Louis's son told an acquaintance, "but he's not tremendously outgoing. It's really funny, because most people with what I would term charisma tend to be fairly outgoing, fairly vivacious."

One day in January 1966, Punchy telephoned Mrs. Louis in Los Angeles. "I'd like to come out to Denver to ski at Aspen," he said.

"It's all right with me, if your mother knows about it."

"I'll clear it with her," the boy said.

A while later, he called back. Everything was arranged.

"I'll fly to Denver, and I'll meet you there," Mrs. Louis said.

So Punchy came to Denver, and Martha Louis was pleased because she believed he had earned a vacation during the break between semesters at Boston University. She gave him $100 to defray his expenses at Aspen, but the next morning the boy's mother called from Chicago.

"All hell broke loose," Mrs. Louis was to say later. "Punchy had left Boston. She was screaming her head off that he had to fly back to Boston to get his clothes. So he came and handed me the money back and said, 'Well, I messed up.' I told him not to lose his head, that everything happens for a reason. 'Don't get discouraged,' I told him."

When the boy returned to Denver from Boston, he drove up to Boulder in the chill of a winter's day and found a cool reception at the University of Colorado. Transfer students would be accepted only if they had been in good standing at their previous schools.

"I'll tell you what we're going to do," Martha Louis told her stepson. "We're going to California."

No sooner had they arrived in Los Angeles than there was another call from Chicago. "Marva was screaming her head off," Martha remembers. "I didn't tell Punchy the things she said 'cause he's quite a little man and he stands his ground. So I talked to Marva later and told her that if Punchy goes back to Chicago he will be reminded of his failure because everybody knows he's supposed to be in Boston University. I said nobody in California knows particularly, nobody cares. I said let him stay with me, and he will find himself."

Louis was not in Los Angeles, but when he called on the phone, Martha told him, "Don't go on radio or television and say your son is in Boston University. Just skip it because people in Boston will know he isn't. He's here with me."

"I just went on a show yesterday and said he was in Boston," Louis said.

A short time later, Louis came home. Martha told him that Punchy had enrolled in the extension school at the University of California, Los Angeles, and was living in their apartment.

Louis scowled. He said, "It's just another one of your responsibilities you went out and got."

"What do you mean, Joe?" Martha demanded. "This is not just another responsibility I went out and gathered up. Since you're taking that attitude I'm going to tell you the truth. Punchy has left Boston. You'd better not say anything to him. He's at the crossroads and at this point needs more understanding and love than he's ever needed before in his life."

Louis's reaction was predictable. A circumstance unrelated to his son's predicament was the cause of his grumbling. Some weeks earlier he had become associated with Muhammad Ali, formerly Cassius Clay, the heavyweight champion of the world. Newspaper reporters inferred from this that Louis simply saw his association with Ali as an opportunity to get back into boxing, again to be a part of a sport in which he had once prospered. Black militancy was not his aspiration. Working with Ali, being around with him in the gymnasium, was just a job for which Louis was paid $1,500.

"What did you do with the money?" Martha asked her husband.

"Spent it," he said.

"How could you goof off?" she demanded. "I've got Punchy here going to school. I've got a lot of obligations. The least you could do was to send some of the money home."

Louis shrugged. Martha turned on him. "I'll tell you what we're going to do, we're going to call a press conference and you're going to tell the newspapers that you're not with the Black Muslims or Cassius Clay."

The newsmen came to the Louises' pleasant apartment and there, against a background of cheerful domesticity, Martha served coffee while Louis disavowed any connection with the Black Muslims. At least this was settled. But his son's academic problem persisted. Although Punchy was at UCLA, he was merely an "extension" student with little or no hope of matriculation. Eventually, Martha arranged for him to have an interview at Denver University. He flew to Denver alone, fretful and frustrated, and was interviewed by the dean of admissions. It was an agreeable meeting. The boy summoned the resources of a charming personality and told his story. He was accepted as a probationary student in the summer session.

"Punchy did so well in summer school," Martha remembers, "they accepted him as a matriculated student.

He graduated on time. Marva came out for his graduation and everybody was happy. He hasn't looked back since."

He went into the National Guard and spent six months at a training camp. By the time he returned home, in November 1969, freshman classes at law school had started. He decided to get a job and to attend law classes. This caused some disquiet in the family. His parents wanted him to concentrate on his studies, but he was pleased with the combination of work and study. Only the stories he heard from Martha Louis about his father's frequently irrational behavior caused him concern. And when a decision was made to commit his father to the Colorado Psychiatric Hospital, the application for commitment was signed by Joseph Louis Barrow, Jr.

"I couldn't help thinking of Arthur Miller's play *Death of a Salesman,*" he said subsequently. "In the play the man's name was Willy Loman, wasn't it? Well, there's a correlation between them. Wasn't Willy a grand guy, just like my father, and then he started growing old and losing his customers? He was never really aware that he had lost his territory. That's the tragedy of it, just like my father's."

3

Like his son, Joe Louis could find in his own father's history a source of dismay. He was only two years old, in 1916, when his father was led away to the Searcy State Hospital for the Insane, a melancholy man defeated by life in a sharecropper's shack off a dirt road that runs between Lafayette and Cusseta in Chambers County, Alabama. The hospital at Mt. Vernon was to be Munroe Barrow's haven for the rest of his life. By the time he died, in his fifty-ninth year, his son had accomplished great deeds in boxing, none of which were recorded in his mind. Munroe Barrow had been a big man, standing six feet three inches and weighing more than 200 pounds, but he had worn himself out trying to support a large family on the meager proceeds from a cotton patch which backed on the ramshackle, crowded hut in which the numerous Barrows somehow found accommodations.

Once, Louis remembers, the shack was owned by Peter Sheley, his mother's uncle. No proof of this exists, nor is it possible to delineate clearly Louis's lineage. His father's father was Lon Barrow, a plantation slave. His grandmother was Victoria Harp Barrow, a slave on a plantation owned by one James Harp. She was supposed to be half Cherokee Indian. Louis remembers all this as hearsay.

What he does know as fact is that his mother, who was Lillie Reese, was born in Chambers Country, in red-clay country, halfway down the map of Alabama, where Georgia backs into it. "She was a good woman," Louis says of her. "She worked hard for us. She was Baptist all her life and brought us all up Baptist."

She had given Munroe Barrow eight children, and the second youngest, born May 13, 1914, was named for his father's brother-in-law, Joe Louis Nichols. He weighed nine pounds at birth. The morning he was born, Susan Radford, a midwife, attended his mother in the unpainted, sagging shack. His brothers and sisters were out in the cotton patch, where they toiled from sunrise to sunset.

Memory of his childhood in Alabama always sets a stable of memories racing in Louis—a winning smile comes over his usually immobile face, leading to an unexpected willingness to talk about his early days.

"My mother," he says, "always told me I was a worse crybaby than my brothers and sisters. When she took a stick to me, I hollered louder than the other kids. And I took a long time walking, the way she told it. I was almost

[17]

a year old before I could get around. I was stubborn in school. My teacher used to make me say words over and over again. I didn't like it. The other kids didn't have to do it. Maybe that's why, when I was coming up in boxing, I didn't like to talk too much. Still don't. A man that has something to say can say it in a couple of words. He don't need all week to make his point."

When Louis was six years old, the family moved to Mount Sinai, a hamlet deeper in Alabama's Buckalew Mountains. By this time his mother had married Pat Brooks, a widower who had five children of his own.

In Mount Sinai the family of fifteen was compressed into a gray plank house on the Waltons' plantation near the town of Waverly. Louis was forced to sleep three in a bed and often rebelled against this form of crowding. But what he remembers especially was how cold it was in the Buckalew Mountains. The kids did not wear shoes and were required to save their good clothes for Sundays. By then, Louis was in school and his sister Eulalia would escort him and his younger sister, Vunies, to classes in the Mount Sinai Baptist Church.

When Eulalia would leave them at the church, Vunies would go into the school. Louis, however, would run into a nearby swamp and hunt what he called "join-y" snakes. It was folklore that these snakes would join together and become whole again even after they were cut apart. Summer was really his time for fun. His stepbrother Pat Brooks was his constant companion. They were of the same age and found a community of interest. They played baseball and liked to lie in the cotton when it went to the cotton gin in a mule-drawn wagon.

On Saturdays, Mr. Brooks would take the kids into
the town of Camp Hill in adjoining Tallapoosa County.
They would look forward to these trips because Camp Hill
had a store-lined main street and it would be fun just to
sit on the wagon and observe the busy scene. Louis was
not aware of racial tension in the back country. Not once,
he insists, did he hear talk of lynching or the difficulties
of being a black man in the Alabama of his youth. He
played with white children; and while he was aware of
differences, he took them as a matter of course. He was
perhaps the least bellicose of all the kids in the family,
certainly less given to arguments than the others. Without
stressing it, he remembers that he once had a fight with
another boy in the school yard. When the teacher saw the
fracas through the school window, she rushed out and
separated them. For some reason, she chose to whip Louis
as an act of discipline. He never understood why. "Guess
I was bigger," he says.

At home, when there was a need for discipline,
Louis's stepfather would speak softly before applying the
hand. He was left-handed and hit hard; and while he was
disinclined to strike out at the children, he imposed pun-
ishment on them equally. He would just as soon lay a hand
on young Pat Brooks as he would on Joe Louis Barrow.

For the most part, life in the gray plank house was
happy. Though food was not abundant, the fare was var-
ied. Fish, bacon, chicken, corn, and potatoes found their
way to the table and were devoured by the hard-working
family. Only the nights were dull. Kerosene lamps fur-
nished the only light in the shack, and the shadows they

threw imposed an ambiance of half-dark brooding. But by the time the sun came up in the morning, the family was back in the crops, toiling to keep the cotton growing, bending their backs to assure themselves of a reasonable share of the proceeds after the landlord took his portion.

By the time Louis was twelve years old, in 1926, word came down to Alabama that Henry Ford was paying good money to factory hands in Detroit. A smile flowered on Pat Brooks's face when he heard of the economic salvation awaiting him in the North. Not too many weeks passed before he was living with a relative on Macomb Street on Detroit's East Side.

"We went up after him," Louis remembers. "The place we lived in on Macomb Street was crowded, but it had something we didn't have in Alabama, an inside toilet. And there were electric lights. It was nice."

When Pat Brooks finally found a job at Ford, the family moved into a frame tenement on Catherine Street. Louis was enrolled in the Duffield School, but it was a waste of time. He was older than the others in his class, and much taller, and he was embarrassed by a stammer he had developed earlier in Alabama. A teacher suggested that he would fare better in a trade school.

"He's going to have to make a living with his hands," said Miss Vada Schwader. "He'd better start now."

At the Bronson Trade School, Louis learned how to use the tools of a cabinetmaker. He made tables and knick-knack closets, and when he brought them home, they augmented the meager furnishings his mother had been able to collect. By then the Depression was on and Pat Brooks had lost his job at Ford. The family went on home relief, and an aimlessness born of despair overcame Louis.

He spent long hours running with the Catherine Street gang and got into fights. Concerned, his mother thought he ought to take violin lessons to take his mind off fighting in the streets. She enrolled him with a teacher on Woodward Avenue, the main drag, but the cultural movement did not take hold. Louis had five or six lessons and quit.

What happened was that he began putting on gloves with the other boys in the Bronson School gymnasium. One afternoon, he knocked out a Mexican lad with one left hook and caught the eye of Thurston McKinney, who was several grades ahead of him in the school. McKinney, an excellent amateur boxer, told Louis, "Get into the amateurs, man. You're a pretty good fighter."

At the time, it was the procedure in amateur boxing to give participants checks which they could cash in for merchandise. The maximum check would provide $25 in merchandise, the minimum $7. The proposal attracted Louis. He followed McKinney's advice.

The first step Louis took was to join the Brewster Recreation Center. His mother, who still was under the impression that he was taking violin lessons, provided the dues he had to pay at Brewster's, believing the money was going to the violin instructor. Louis long ago forgot the name of the violin teacher, but he does remember his first boxing coach.

"Fellow's name was Atler Ellis," Louis says. "He was the first man showed me how to hold my hands up. He taught me a lot about boxing."

Even then, for a while, it appeared that Louis would

not pursue the sport. He quit school and got a job for $25 a week at the Briggs auto-body plant. It was muscle-tiring labor that diminished his interest in boxing and the need for daily training sessions.

"I pushed truck bodies to the sprayer on the assembly line," he explained, long after he had won the world heavyweight championship. "The tape would come off the body covers and land on the floor sticky side up. The tape would gum onto the dolly wheels, and you'd get a real workout pushing those truck bodies. I would leave the factory around five o'clock, go home for dinner. Working that hard kind of made me forget about boxing."

Saturday, his day off, was devoted to boxing. He would go to Brewster's and pull on the gloves and go into the ring with anybody who wanted a workout.

Louis's first formal bout would have discouraged any other lad. He does not remember the exact date it happened—either in November 1932 or in early 1933—but he does know that the place of his boxing baptism was the Edison Athletic Club in Detroit. It was a mismatch. Louis's opponent was Johnny Miler, an experienced amateur who had represented the United States in the 1932 Olympic Games at Los Angeles. Miler knocked Louis down seven times in two rounds. Not even the $7 merchandise check assuaged the pain in Louis's body and psyche. Unhappily, he dragged himself home. He gave the merchandise check to his mother.

For the next six months, Louis stayed away from the gym. He switched jobs and went to work in the Ford plant at River Rouge. Later, when he was earning large purses in boxing and spending it as quickly as it came in, he said,

"I worked in the 'B' building at Ford's. My time card is still there. If things get tough, I can always go back."

It must never be forgotten that the black man's economic status in Detroit during the Depression was controlled by an undercurrent of ever-threatening doom. Louis's stepfather was aware of this and quietly encouraged his stepson to stay at Ford, to be grateful for a job in hand instead of a vision of riches won in the ring. But the young man was fed by an insistent, demanding urge to get going in boxing. He had found, in the ring, a way to express himself, to assert his individuality. His mother told him, "Joe, if you want to keep on boxing, you keep on with it. I'll work for you to get it."

The words were music to Louis's ears and sung him into a happier humor. He went back to Brewster's and began training again, this time under the direction of Holman Williams, a professional middleweight fighter. Williams showed Louis how to move in the ring and expressed optimism about the young fighter's future in boxing. "Just you keep working at it," he said. "It ain't easy, but it's worth it."

One night, at the Forest Athletic Club in Detroit, Louis had his second amateur bout. The fight encompassed two punches, both landed by Louis. It was his first knockout. He was jubilant and couldn't wait until he reached home to give his mother the $25 merchandise check he had been awarded as a winner. There were many more checks after this. In a two-year career as an amateur, Louis had fifty-four fights. Forty-three of his fifty victories were scored by knockout. He weighed about 170 pounds and fought among the light heavyweights. There was, in the midst of this early success, a night of disappointment. It came in a fight with a former Notre Dame football player named Max Marek and involved the light-heavy-weight championship of the Amateur Athletic Union. For the first two rounds, the two fought on even terms, but Marek came along in the third round and outboxed Louis. He was awarded the decision.

There were several reasons for Louis's defeat. The simplest was that Marek was too strong for him. Another concerned Louis's eating habits. Steak is a staple of a fighter's diet. In its place Louis ate frankfurters and gorged himself on ice cream and apple pie. Nevertheless, Louis did win the novice light-heavyweight championship of the Golden Gloves in his first year as an amateur. Later, opposing Stanley Evans in another bout, Louis was defeated decisively. He had, before the fight, eaten a frank-furter and a large slice of apple pie.

By then, Louis had switched gymnasiums. He was training now at the Detroit Amateur Club, where George Moody was in charge. Moody was to play a catalytic role in Louis's future. Early in 1934, after Louis had defeated Evans in a return bout in the Detroit Golden Gloves, Moody introduced him to John Roxborough, a meeting that marked a major alteration in Louis's life.

Roxborough was active in Negro affairs in Detroit. That he also was a numbers operator was overlooked in the context of the times. He was a forceful figure in the Young Negroes Progressive Association and the Urban League, and people in the black community regarded him as a completely worthwhile man whose work in behalf of his race was quietly done and usually effective. He was soft of voice and mood, and early gained from Louis a measure of respect that never declined.

"I'll tell you what I'll do for you," Roxborough told the young fighter. "You come to live with me in my house. You'll eat right and sleep right, and I'll make sure you get some good clothes. What do you say?"

Louis went home and discussed the proposal with his mother and stepfather. There was full unemployment in the household, and the family was on home relief. The invitation for Louis to live at Roxborough's place was accepted.

Life bloomed for the young amateur fighter. Some of Roxborough's expensive clothes were altered to fit him. He ate with his new mentor, who also provided $5 a week for pocket money. He went into the ring draped in a splendid terrycloth robe; and instead of wearing old bandages to protect his hands against injury, he wrapped his fists in new bandages for each fight. His old tennis sneakers were replaced by leather boxing shoes.

Finally, on June 12, 1934, Joe Louis engaged in his last bout as an amateur. Appropriately, it took place in Detroit, in an intercity tournament. His opponent, Joe Bauer, a Clevelander, lasted just one round. Louis hit him with a left to the jaw and a right just above his cheekbone. It was over within ninety seconds.

Even before the fight, Roxborough had anticipated the dynamics of Louis's inevitable role in boxing. The young man was outstanding and there was every prospect of his success. But Roxborough was aware of a recurring rumor in the black community regarding a Negro's opportunities in boxing, especially in the heavyweight division.

A black heavyweight could not get many matches, and when he did, he was usually committed to defeat by obligation.

While the more sophisticated were skeptical of Roxborough's design for Louis, the man himself was determined that Louis would have every chance to fulfill his apparent ability as a fighter. Louis was in his nonage, only twenty years old, and Roxborough had to gain his mother's consent before he could sign any contracts in behalf of the young man. So he went to see Joe's mother, and they discussed Louis's future. "You take him, keep him a good boy," she said. "You'll do fine for him."

Up in Chicago, Roxborough's friend Julian Black was dabbling in boxing. They had been associated in various business deals, and it was in Black's direction that Roxborough looked for help. In June 1934 he took Louis to Chicago to talk with Black. An agreement was reached: Louis would turn professional under the guidance of the two men. Jack Blackburn was hired as trainer.

In his time as a fighter, Blackburn had been defined as a foremost lightweight, though he had not become a champion. He had been involved in a fatal knife fight in Philadelphia and had, from 1909 to 1913, done time for manslaughter. When his career in the ring was finished in 1923, he became a trainer and produced two world champions—Bud Taylor, bantamweight, and Sammy Mandell, lightweight.

Louis stayed in Chicago and lived in a rented room on Forty-sixth Street near South Parkway. He soon learned to respect Blackburn. "He called me 'Chappie' and I called him 'Chappie,'" Louis would say later.

"Whatever he told me to do in the ring, I did. I used to be clumsy-footed when I was a kid in Alabama. When I began with Blackburn, he saw things I didn't know about myself. He saw I couldn't follow a left hook with a right without picking up one foot. He said it was no good, that a fighter had to keep both feet planted on the canvas to get power, or to take a punch. He soon had me throwing a series of punches. He was the best teacher anybody ever had."

In Chicago, Louis no longer ate hot dogs. The room in which he lived was in the apartment of Bill Bottoms. He was a chef, and he cooked for Louis. Later, he was the cook in Louis's training camp. Blackburn was a stern trainer, and he looked the part. A bony face, marked by a scar on the left cheek and set off by beady eyes that peered out of angular slits, he appeared as an instrument of discipline. Usually taciturn, he was informative and kindly where Louis was involved. He knew boxing as a serious business and instilled in his pupil an early devotion to the course undertaken in Chicago. Louis's career as a professional fighter was about to begin, and he could not have been in more efficient hands. He was mostly pleased and often happy, yet within the cauldron of his mind boiled the influences that were to lead, years later, to dark despair.

4

Martha Louis was determined to conceal from her neighbors the sight of her husband being led away to the Colorado Psychiatric Hospital. She cautioned the Denver Sheriff's Department, "Come in the back way, through the garage that leads into the kitchen. That way, nobody will see you. There'll be no fuss."

In outlining the situation, she explained, "The way the house is laid out, with the wide, grassy setback from the street, there's no driveway in front, and you can't block anybody's view. If Joe does offer any opposition, it would be a great mess outside in front."

She was not going to be at home. She had arranged

to spend that Friday, May 1, 1970, at the home of a cousin who was a registered nurse. Neither Louis's son nor daughter would be there. With variations, each had made arrangements to be elsewhere. In regard to Punchy, this was mandatory: it was a working day at the bank.

In their places, Martha had asked the Reverend Carl Walker to stay with Joe. When he had been a divinity student, the minister had lived with the Louises. He felt at home in the place and Louis accepted his presence without suspicion or resentment. In order to keep himself occupied, Reverend Walker even set himself to the task of mopping the floor and putting things in order.

The week had been a busy one for Mrs. Louis. When she had prevailed upon her husband to come to Denver with her, she had done so in the belief that he might find some relief from his anxieties in the pleasant surroundings of their home. Then, on the first night there, Louis had torn apart the lamp in his bedroom. It was a sign too valid to dismiss.

She went to see Dr. John H. MacDonald, chief of forensic psychiatry at Colorado General Hospital. His reputation had been known to her even before her arrival in Denver.

"This is a serious matter," Mrs. Louis told Dr. Mac-Donald. "I think it is an urgent matter."

A lengthy discussion of Louis's illness took place. "But I must tell you one thing," Mrs. Louis said, "Joe doesn't believe he is sick. So it is going to be impossible to get him to come here to see you. Would it be possible to have you come to our house for a consultation?"

When Dr. MacDonald consented to this arrangement, Mrs. Louis went to see Stephen L. R. McNichols, a former governor of Colorado. "McNichols," she told an acquaintance, "was an old friend. I felt that it would be easier if he came to the house with Dr. MacDonald. Joe wouldn't be so apprehensive, knowing McNichols was there."

The meeting took place in the living room. Joe sat on a Louis XV couch set against a long wall on which there was hung a picture of him in fighting garb. The picture was in contrast to the melancholy man on the couch. The years had touched him harshly. He was baldish, and his eyes, once so firmly on target in the ring, now moved apprehensively in a jowl-hung face. His visitors confronted him from across the room.

Before long, jovial greetings deteriorated into searching examination. Louis began tracing his labyrinthian delusions and indicated a firm resistance to a program of psychiatric attention. After forty-five minutes, Dr. Mac-Donald and McNichols left.

"I could hardly wait until I heard from Dr. Mac-Donald," Martha Louis said. "I couldn't ask him what he thought in front of Joe, so I waited awhile and then called him on the phone. He said the only thing he could tell me was to make a move in a hurry for my sake as well as Joe's because Joe was a very sick man."

There was only one direction in which Martha Louis could go. She had read the compass of law in Colorado pertaining to mental illness and knew the way the needle pointed. Under the law, it was possible, upon verification by qualified physicians, to obtain from the probate court an order to hospitalize for a period of up to three months any person deemed in need of psychiatric treatment.

Now, armed with a letter from Dr. MacDonald, Martha Louis went about the task of obtaining a court order committing Louis to the Colorado Psychiatric Hospital "for observation, diagnosis, and treatment for mental illness for a period not to exceed three months unless extended by further order of the court."

Martha, accompanied by Punchy and Jacqueline, went to the office of the city attorney in the City and County Building. They had agreed that all of them would sign the application for the motion and order to hospitalize Louis.

Martha Louis said, "I felt—my original idea was—that the three of us would sign the petition because of Joe being who he was and nobody wanting to be blamed that this was a vindictive thing."

When they were in the city attorney's office, appearing before Albert Eckhardt, assistant city attorney in the Mental Health Division, he looked up from their application and asked, "Who is going to sign this?"

"We all are," Martha Louis said.

"One signature will do," Eckhardt said.

"I'll sign," young Joe said.

"But why should you have all the responsibility?" Jacqueline asked.

"My shoulders are broad, if they want to blame me," he replied, not without a show of determination. "Dad's in need of help. I know he needs help. And I'm going to sign."

The application went to Judge David Brofman of the probate court. Attached to it was Dr. MacDonald's letter, plus letters from Dr. Robert C. Bennett and Dr. James Ellison, both of Detroit. Judge Brofman, in chambers, then signed the motion and order to hospitalize the former heavyweight champion of the world. Haste was implicit in the legal document.

It directed "the sheriff of the City and County of Denver to pick up the respondent at 2675 Monaco Parkway or wherever he may be found in the City and County of Denver and deliver respondent to Colorado Psychiatric Hospital, FORTHWITH."

There was no need to doubt that Louis was at home. He had not gone out since his arrival from Los Angeles earlier in the week. The day was slightly overcast. Topcoat weather, a court attendant said. When the Sheriff Department's auto arrived in the common driveway in back of Louis's house, Reverend Walker was prepared to admit the visitors—three uniformed deputy sheriffs and Mose Trujillo, a liaison officer of the probate court.

"He's in the front part of the house," Reverend Walker explained. "I'll tell him you're here."

The court officer and the deputy sheriffs remained in the kitchen. The deputies were in uniform, with their guns in belt holsters, each apprehensive because none knew just how Louis would react to their presence and the nature of their assignment.

In a moment Louis, obviously distressed, confronted them. He told Trujillo he would not leave unless he was permitted to call the White House first.

"I know Nixon, I want to tell the President what you are doing," Louis asserted.

He went to the telphone and put a call through to

Washington, D.C. But when he asked for the President, he was told that he could talk to a White House aide but not directly to Mr. Nixon.

"Okay, then I got to call all the newspapers and radio and TV stations," he told the men who had come to take him away. "I want everybody to know what you are doing to me."

By this time there was an outbreak of confusion. In the presence of the great Joe Louis, there was a bending to his wishes. He phoned the *Denver Post* and the *Rocky Mountain News*. Before long, cameramen and reporters filled the rather small living room. Abruptly, two other newcomers were in the house; somebody had summoned Irving P. Andrews, Louis's attorney in Denver, and Truman Coles, the public defender. Coles acted quickly. He advised Louis not to talk to the reporters. Then, aware that Louis was under legal restraint, Andrews advised his client to prepare himself for the trip to the hospital.

Louis had been wearing sun-tan trousers and a white sport shirt. He packed a small leather bag, went to the refrigerator for an apple and bit into it. He donned a topcoat. Having surrendered, in a sense, he nodded that he was ready to go to the hospital. He went out the back way, through the garage, and into the deputy sheriff's car. The ride to the hospital, past the University of Colorado medical complex, was uneventful. He was assigned to a semiprivate room.

By then, news of Louis's hospitalization and the circumstances under which it had been accomplished was being broadcast on radio and television. Martha Louis was in a rage. She had made every effort to effect Louis's removal to the hospital quietly, but it had not worked out that way. "I am very peeved with the Sheriff's Department," she said when the news broke. "I felt that the only thing they had was an order that they were duty-bound, as officers, to carry out. But because of it being Joe, of course, they catered to him in every way. And after they were in the house and the damage was done, one guy who was in charge of the detail got on the phone and apologized to me. He told me he didn't realize Joe was as sick as he was, and he was sorry the thing had gotten out of hand. I said, 'Big deal, you're sorry now.' I said, 'Had the judge not had good grounds for issuing the order, he would not have issued it.' "

Five days later, Louis was transferred to the Veterans Administration Hospital, a few blocks from the Colorado Psychiatric Hospital, on Clermont Street. He was given a private room on the seventh floor of the red-brick building, just off Seven North, a ward in the charge of Dr. Gary C. Martin, a young, bearded psychiatrist.

Louis underwent immediate physical examination. What it disclosed, in a medical phrase, "was essentially unremarkable except for blood pressure of 180/120, a well-healed gallbladder surgery scar, and a few internal hemorrhoidal tags." Psychological testing essentially disclosed "no organicity"—ruling out the possibility of brain damage as a result of Louis's long years of combat in the ring. A diagnosis of involutional depressive reaction, paranoid type, excluding any evidence of a thought disorder, was confirmed.

Three months after Louis's arrival at the hospital, a visitor sat with him on a lawn used as an eighteen-hole putting course. For the sixth week in succession, Louis had just won a putting contest among the patients of Seven North. First prize was $2. In 1946, Louis had collected a purse of $591,116.44 for knocking out Billy Conn. The reward for winning the putting contest seemed to please him almost as much. He appeared relaxed and sociable.

Imagining the dismay that revelations in print might cause Louis, the visitor asked, "How do you feel about the book being written about you?"

"I don't want to hide anything. Tell it like it is," the former champion said.

5

During the summer of Louis's first year as a professional he made a rewarding discovery: he liked
training, even roadwork. Blackburn would call for him at
Bill Bottoms's place at six o'clock in the morning. Together, they would go to Washington Park, where Louis
would run three miles while the trainer waited for him
outside. Then, roadwork finished, Louis would return to
the apartment and go back to bed. In those days, unmo-
lested by demons, he could sleep even while standing.

At eleven o'clock he would get out of bed, have
breakfast, and then wait around until he was ready to go
to George Trafton's Gymnasium. He would loosen up by

shadow boxing and then pull on sixteen-ounce sparring gloves and go into the ring. Blackburn never strayed too far. The trainer's gimlet eye followed every movement Louis made in the gym, in or out of the ring. He showed Louis how to shadow box while looking into a large perpendicular mirror. In this way, Louis could see for himself just what he was doing with his fists. Blackburn stressed balance. "You're falling over when you throw the hook," he told the young fighter. "You've got to be in a position to throw a follow-up right, or to block a counterpunch after you throw your right." Louis worked hard on combination punching, which was to become the mark of his awesome ability as a fighter—hard, brown arms driving two iron fists, a human machine harnessed for destructive power, inevitably victorious.

Louis was not matched carelessly in his early fights. Mostly aware that they were strangers in a white man's sport, Roxborough and Black cautiously appraised each opponent to make certain that he did not represent an entrapment for their young hero. They had, after all, made an investment in Louis; and while there was every prospect of profit, there was no guarantee that his labors in the ring would prove a highly marketable commodity.

By the terms of their agreement, all essential expenditures would be paid out of each purse, after which Louis and his managers would split the pot evenly. Ordinarily, this would have been regarded as a harsh equation. In almost all other instances, expenses would "come off the top," after which the fighter would receive two-thirds of his purse, leaving one-third for his manager. This all seemed academic in the summer of 1934. Louis had not yet had his first professional fight, and the road to riches loomed narrow and winding, even uncharted for a black fighter who had to overcome prejudice on all sides.

Consider the times: major league baseball was truly the nation's major sport. No Negro wore a major league uniform. And the prospect of a black heavyweight champion was anathema. Although nineteen years had passed since Jack Johnson had been knocked out by Jess Willard, connotations of Johnson's reign as heavyweight champion were still strong. He had made the unpardonable mistake of letting life take him where it would, even frequently into the arms of white women. His egregious mistake, the more sophisticated believed, was that he had asserted himself against whites in the ring, had, in fact, proved almost invincible until the last, forlorn gesture against Willard under suspicious circumstances and a hot sun on an April afternoon in Havana in 1915.

Louis had engaged in only a few fights when he was introduced to Johnson in Detroit. He knew of Johnson's reputation as a smart fighter and stood in awe of him. Whatever else Johnson was remembered for did not concern Louis, who did not scorn anybody because of the color of his skin or the pattern of his behavior. People warned him against Johnson's mistakes. Louis said, "Every man's got a right to his own mistakes. Ain't no man that ain't made any."

In their choice of Louis's early opponents, Roxborough and Black chose fighters of equal experience and lesser motivation. His rivals were, on the face of it, all vulnerable to Louis's powerful punching. Because of his reputation as an amateur, Louis's first professional bout was a main event. It took place at Bacon Casino in Chicago on July 4, 1934. His opponent was Jack Kracken, a local heavyweight. Louis went out at the opening bell and followed Blackburn's orders. He worked on Kracken's midsection. Kracken dropped his hands to protect his stomach. Louis landed a left hook to his opponent's jaw. Kracken went down and was counted out. Only two minutes of the first round had passed. The purse came to $52, not enough to interest the managers. They permitted Louis to keep the entire purse. He sent most of it home to his mother. A week later there was another knockout, this one in three rounds. Louis's purse for knocking out Willie Davis came to $2 more than he had received for his first fight.

Next, Larry Udell went down for the full count in another Chicago arena, Marigold Gardens. For two rounds of action Louis was paid $101. Two weeks later he went into the ring with Jack Kranz. The bout was scheduled for eight rounds, but nobody expected Kranz to go the distance. He did. "Don't worry," Blackburn said. "Fights like that give you experience. You can't knock them all out." The next time out, Louis flattened Buck Everett in two rounds.

By now, promoters in Detroit were clamoring for Louis's services. They knew he would draw a large crowd in his home town. Roxborough arranged for him to fight in the Naval Armory in Detroit. He knocked out Alex Borchuk in the fourth round, but the fight was memorable for another reason: Borchuk hit Louis so hard Joe has never forgotten the effect of the punch. It landed flush on the jaw in the second round and broke one of his molars.

[39]

The pain was excruciating. In the corner, Blackburn told him, "It's your own fault. You should have been inside the hook." After the fight, which had been broadcast on radio, Louis went home to see his mother. She had taken the broadcast in stride. "They never knew how close I came to losing," Louis said.

After each victory, while his hand was being raised by the ring announcer, Louis remained expressionless. Not that he found boxing a melancholy task. His facial immobility indicated neither balefulness nor unconcern. He was simply impassive, though sportswriters read menace into his impassivity. They wrote in glowing terms about his physical proportions, which made as remarkable an impression as his face. His muscles, deeply buried beneath smooth brown skin, gave every promise of harnessed power. Only his buttocks and thighs appeared heavy, but the movements of his hands were so quick they disguised the relative slowness of his feet. He was still growing, approaching 190 pounds, and not yet twenty-one, but already people were beginning to think of him inevitably as a future heavyweight champion.

Within six months, Louis had won a dozen fights, ten by knockout. He was less than a virtuoso, of course, but he was learning to taunt an opponent with a hammerlike jab that eventually struck the core of his object. His left hook was his most powerful weapon, but he did not depend on it alone to flay his opponents. When Adolph Wiater went the scheduled ten rounds with him in Chicago, some reporters scoffed at Louis as a robot who did not react quickly enough to a rival's unexpected movements. "He keeps winning, don't he?" Blackburn insisted.

"Can't ask more from him. He's still learning."

Louis spent the Christmas of 1934 in Detroit. It was a happy homecoming. The family was financially in the clear. Louis had repaid the home relief authorities $270 from a $1,400 purse from one of his bouts. He had enough money to give presents to his mother, brothers, and sisters. And he was beginning to dress like a dude. He wore striped suits mostly. The jackets had wide lapels, and his broad-brimmed hats were usually of a light color. He spent time with Freddy Guinyard. When they were kids, Louis and Guinyard worked on an ice-delivery wagon. Louis was much taller and stronger than Guinyard but not as crafty. Guinyard would stay downstairs guarding the horse and wagon while Louis carried seventy-five pounds of ice up the stairs to a customer's flat. When Louis got together with Guinyard, they would laugh about their days in the ice business. "What's your beef?" Guinyard asked Louis. "I let you carry the ice, and it put muscles on you, didn't it?" Louis bent over in laughter.

There was not much time for laughter after the Christmas vacation of 1934. Within a fortnight, Louis had two more fights. One was against Patsy Perroni in the Olympic Stadium in Detroit. Perroni had been a professional for six years. He was agile and skilled, and made Louis do all the work. Louis came away with a decision. The fans were disappointed. He was not. He got $4,227 for the fight. Not all of it went to him. By then, his managers were taking their share of his purses. They had moved Louis well, and he was absolutely pleased with the financial arrangements. Not once in the cotton patch in Alabama, or toiling at Ford, had he dreamed that he would have so much money at once. Exactly one week after the fight with Perroni, Louis was in the ring again, this time with Hans Birkie in Pittsburgh. He knocked Birkie out in the last round of a ten-round bout.

Louis's last victim before his Christmas vacation had been a Californian named Lee Ramage. Louis had knocked him out in eight rounds; but the fight had been reasonably close, and when promoters in Los Angeles suggested a return bout out there, Roxborough and Black seized the opportunity to take Joe to California for a big outdoor fight at Wrigley Field. For a purse of $3,000, Louis again knocked out Ramage, this time within two rounds.

In Detroit, Scotty Monteith heard about the knock-out of Ramage. He was a promoter who had been in the boxing business for years and was friendly with Rox-borough. He waited until Louis's co-manager returned home and then phoned him.

"The kid can't miss," Monteith said. "He's going to be a champ. He's a bomber."

"Thanks, Scotty," Roxborough said.

"Come to think of it, that boy is a real brown bomber."

The sportswriters picked it up. From then on, Joe Louis was known as the "Brown Bomber."

Promoters from all over the country were importu-nate. Louis's services were in demand everywhere. Rox-borough and Black were not surprised by the suggestions made to them. One New York promoter who controlled the ring in a major arena called Roxborough.

"I can help your boy," the promoter said.

"We can use help," Roxborough replied. "We think Joe is ready for big things."

"Well, you understand he's a nigger, and he can't win every time he goes into the ring."

"So am I," Roxborough said. He hung up.

In New York the boxing world was seething. A year earlier, a Broadway ticket scalper named Mike Jacobs had joined forces with three journalists who worked for William Randolph Hearst and had promoted boxing shows for Mrs. William Randolph Hearst's Free Milk Fund for Babies. They were Edward J. Frayne, sports editor of the *New York American*; Wilston S. ("Bill") Farnsworth, sports editor of the *New York Journal*; and Damon Runyon, a Hearst columnist whose fictionalized Broadway characters were known wherever English was spoken and read.

About Jacobs, it was once written: "Jacobs himself was a curmudgeonish product of the rough-and-tumble life of Broadway, along which he had achieved a reputation as the most resourceful ticket speculator in the theatrical district. He was hard-crusted and crafty and totally without formal education. When he was in need of a favor, he was charming and warm and obliging, almost to the point of sycophancy; otherwise he was a ruthless predator who had struggled up from poverty on New York's lower West Side and had become the foremost promoter of boxing in the world."

For years Madison Square Garden had had a monopolistic hold on big-time boxing. Storming the castle, Jacobs and his cohorts assailed the gates of the Garden in the sweet name of charity. Outwardly, they appeared to be motivated by an unyielding philanthropic compulsion to help Mrs. Hearst's Free Milk Fund for Babies. In their totality, they were a band of self-seekers.

The Garden's boxing promoter was James J. Johnston, a charming man known as the "Boy Bandit," though he was long past his youth. For some years, the Milk Fund had benefited from boxing shows held in Madison Square Garden and in outdoor arenas controlled by the Garden. There came a time when Colonel John Reed Kilpatrick, who was president of the Garden, informed the Milk Fund that he had raised the rental fee for its next boxing show at the Garden. Frayne, Farnsworth, and Runyon accused the Garden of depriving helpless infants of free milk and prevailed upon Jacobs to join them in the organization of a new promotional corporation, the 20th Century Sporting Club.

Jacobs went to Miami Beach to promote a bout between Barney Ross, the junior welterweight champion, and Frankie Klick, a San Franciscan. Ross's managers were Sam Pian and Art Winch. They were Chicagoans and were familiar with the achievements of the young black heavyweight who was winning fight after fight in their town.

"Mike, I got something good for you," Pian said.

"Listen, Mike, this is good," Winch said.

"I got 'nuff troubles with the fight," Jacobs scowled. "I don't need nothing more."

"Mike, there's a kid fighting around Chicago name of Joe Louis you should get," Pian said.

"He's a heavyweight," Winch said. "He'll be a champ."

"We'll see about it," Jacobs said.

When he returned to New York, he conferred with his partners in the 20th Century Sporting Club. Roxborough was contacted. Jacobs went out to Los Angeles to see Louis fight Ramage. He talked to Roxborough and Black; and later, after the fight, he told Louis, "Joe, you can fight on the level when you fight for me. If you win, you win. You don't have to drop a fight to anybody. I'll make a lot of money for you."

Two weeks later, in San Francisco, Louis knocked out Donald ("Reds") Barry in three rounds. The work was not hard and Louis was paid $1,000. It beat working for Ford.

By the time Louis fought Natie Brown in Detroit three weeks after the bout with Barry, the build-up was on. Jacobs invited several dozen New York sportswriters to be his guests in Detroit. He conducted the junket in grand style, transporting the writers on a luxury train and putting them up in a fine hotel. The presence of the eastern "jury" keyed up Louis. Brown, determined to last the scheduled ten rounds, covered up defensively. It was Louis's task to shoot through Brown's guard. In his eagerness to do so, Louis lost poise and punch. He hit Brown ten to one and opened wounds on his opponent's face, but couldn't knock him out. Winning by decision only was a disappointment. The New York sportswriters reacted differently. The stories they sent back East extolled Louis as a potential champion.

Everybody went back to Jacob's hotel suite, where a party was soon in progress. Louis neither drank nor smoked. He sat in an upholstered chair and took in the scene. The merriment pleased him. Later, Jacobs and Roxborough and Black went into another room to talk business. Jacobs produced a contract which would give the 20th Century Sporting Club exclusive rights to Louis's services as a boxer. Roxborough came into the parlor and asked Louis to join the conference. They talked for a long time, trying to make themselves heard above the noise from the other rooms in the suite. When it came time for the contract to be signed, Louis wrote his signature in an inexpert scrawl. He had committed himself to the big town, New York, and he could not help but laugh. The room in which the contract was signed was a toilet.

6

During their courtship, Martha Louis paid no attention to rumors of Joe's associations with other women. They spent most of their time in California, where she pursued her law practice and was too busy to concern herself with Louis's romantic bent. But then a pattern of gossip began to evolve.

Remembering it, she says, "After we got married, I heard different women's names dropped. I heard about Carolle Drake, who was quite a beautiful girl. A model. Her husband once sued Joe for alienation of affection, but he was a minister and the case was settled out of court. That was back in 1950. I heard about a girl up in San

[47]

Francisco and a couple of women in Detroit. One of them, I believe, was named Theresa. Joe was supposed to set her up in business. I heard about any number of women, but none of them was really in the picture as far as I was concerned at the moment. I felt that any women that were in Joe's life prior to my meeting him was no concern of mine."

Another reason for her unconcern, the simplest, was that she believed most of Louis's affairs were of the hit-and-run variety. And she held the firm conviction that her husband's addiction to golf sublimated all other activities. He played every day in Los Angeles, either at the Hillcrest Country Club or the Fox Hills Country Club. Some days he would play eighteen holes at the first club and then travel to the other course for another eighteen-hole round. And, if his game was off, he might buy a bucket of balls and hit them for hours.

"He don't buy no regular balls—no, not Joe Louis—he buys the Select balls, the best, which cost $1.25 a bucket," Martha once told Gay Talese, the author. "And he'll hit, if he's real mad, two, or three, or four bucketfuls, $5 worth. And some nights he comes home, all excited, and says, 'Well, sweetheart, I finally got it today! And all these years playing golf, I just realized what I been doing wrong.' But a day later he may come home, all mad from throwing clubs, and say, 'I'm never gonna play again!' I'll say, 'But, honey, you told me yesterday you had it!' He'll say, 'I had it, but I didn't keep it.' The next morning it might be raining, and I'll say, 'Sweetheart, you gonna play golf today? It's raining.' And he'll say, 'It rains on the

[48]

course, but it don't rain on the players.' And off to the golf course he goes."

Eventually, at least one of Louis's other interests worried her. A new name was added to the roster of females. This one, who shall here be known as Helen Dayton, had been Louis's friend for many years, going back to the days of his championship; and when Martha Louis heard of her, she began asking questions. Proud of her ability as an investigator, Mrs. Louis later recited some of the details.

"Helen Dayton was standing in line with the rest of the girls when Joe Louis was still married to Marva. She was just one of a conglomeration of women around Joe. What Joe saw in her I never could understand, but maybe she had the invisible going for her. I guess she looked good to him."

When Martha asked Louis, "What about Helen Dayton?" she knew she had started a conversation that would displease him.

"A girl I know," he said brusquely.

"You know her a long time. Why didn't you marry her?"

"I didn't want her. If I wanted her, I could have married her."

"That's true," Martha Louis said. "You could have married her after Marva or after Rose. But she seemed to be available anytime you wanted to play."

That, for the moment, ended the subject. "He just wouldn't talk about it," Martha Louis said. "He's that way. Joe would never be abusive, even when you caught him dead to right in a lie. You'd say, 'Look, Joe, this is the way it happened,' and he'd just laugh."

[49]

The wife could not pass off the matter lightly. Indignation thick with jealousy absorbed her. She was determined to learn more about her husband's relationship with Helen Dayton.

At the time, it was Martha Louis's custom to bring him breakfast in bed. She would turn on the television set for him to see a morning talk show, drive to a newsstand to get him the *Los Angeles Times,* and then leave for court. This one morning, Louis appeared jittery.

"What are you going to do today, Joe?" Martha asked him.

"Maybe sit around and look at the World Series game or go out and see it someplace else."

"I'll see you later," Martha said.

Driving out to court in suburban Los Angeles, she speculated about her husband's behavior that morning. Why had he been so jittery? For most of the morning and afternoon she was occupied with a legal case in which she was counsel. Then, abruptly, the thought came to her, "Helen's in town."

She rushed to a telephone and called the Beverly Hilton Hotel. Yes, Miss Dayton was registered, but the operator could not disclose the number of her room. She drove to the hotel and went to the reception desk. The clerk was as tight-lipped as the operator.

Martha Louis put her faith in further investigation. She left the lobby of the hotel and entered the florist's shop.

"I want to send some flowers to a friend in the hotel," she said. "She's registered, but I don't have her room number. Can you get it for me?"

The florist called the reception desk and was given the number of Helen Dayton's room. "I think it was 417," Martha Louis remembers. "I sent the flowers and went home." She waited outside the house for Louis to arrive. When he got out of a cab, she greeted him. "How's room 417?" she said. Louis wasn't flustered.

"You a regular Dick Tracy," he said.

7

The spring of 1935 was a happy one for Louis. In the interval between signing with Jacobs and finally going to New York, his name took on new and brighter meaning nationally. The sports pages carried lengthy stories about him and pictures of him appeared in Sunday newspaper supplements. Consequently, as Louis recalls, he could not walk down a street in Chicago or Detroit without people gathering around him. "It was like being a governor or a mayor, or something like that," he says. "I wasn't used to it, but I don't say I didn't like it."

He was approaching his twenty-first birthday and his life had become a sequence of agreeable events. He had, only lately, paid $9,000 outright for the purchase of a house for his mother on McDougall Avenue in Detroit. Another $2,500 went for repairs, and the furnishings, including a piano and radio, cost $3,000. In addition, he had made down payments on two other houses, one for his sisters Susie and Emmarell and another, in Wayne, Michigan, for his stepbrother Pat Brooks. And he was driving his own car. It was a Ford, presented to him by John Roxborough.

His workouts in George Trafton's gym were strengthening muscles and refining skills. Blackburn talked to him about his failure to knock out Natie Brown. "You got to use a can opener on fellers that cover up like that," the old trainer said. Louis asked, "What's that?" The old trainer threw an uppercut. "That'll open 'em up," he said.

Louis went into the ring with Roy Lazer in Chicago and knocked him out in the third round. His pay was $12,000, almost twice as much as he had received for the bout with Brown. By his twenty-first birthday, he had added four more knockouts to his record. It was time for him to go to New York to fight Primo Carnera.

When Louis's train pulled into Grand Central Station, newsmen of every stripe were assembled there. All of the city's newspapers were represented, along with reporters from the wire services. Newsreel photographers pushed newspaper photographers around in their frenzy to get the best shots from the right angles. He had drawn unusual numbers of reporters in Chicago and Detroit and Los Angeles, but nothing to compare with the outpouring in New York. Naturally taciturn, he could not find words fast enough to reply to the newsmen's questions. Some reporters wrote that he was sulky. "I was a kid then," he said later. "It takes a lot of experience to handle a thing like that."

Louis was kept busy. He was taken down to City Hall to meet Mayor LaGuardia. He did a boxing act on the stage of the Harlem Opera House. He met Jack Dempsey in Jacobs's offices in the Forrest Hotel, off Broadway, and talked about boxing. "I was glad to meet Dempsey," he said. "I knew about him and wanted to be a good puncher like him."

Roxborough and Black were occupied in other areas. Their major task was to complete the contracts for Louis's first fight in New York, at Yankee Stadium on the night of June 25, 1935. Carnera had come from Italy some years before. He was six feet six inches tall and weighed about 250 pounds. He was owned and operated by a New York mob led by Owney Madden, an influential gangster. Regarded as a feeble fighter, he had, in one of boxing's many curious developments, become heavyweight champion by knocking out Jack Sharkey. But at the time he was to meet Louis, he was a former champion. Max Baer had knocked him out to take the title.

All seemed serene on the surface during Louis's first days in New York. Beneath it there was a seething strain involving the management of Louis. One night several members of Madden's mob encountered Louis's managers in a Harlem nightclub. They tried to buy a piece of the fighter's contract. One of them told Roxborough, "You're a nigger manager and got a nigger fighter. You ain't going no place in New York without us." Roxborough and

Black resisted the suggestion. Still later, a gang of jewel thieves approached Roxborough with another proposition. They would give him $50,000 to cut them in on his fighter. "He's not for sale," Roxborough said. There was gangland pressure on all sides. A leader of the Purple Gang in Detroit finally opened a valve. He phoned Roxborough and said, "Don't worry, John. We do business with those people in New York. They do things for us, we do things for them. They won't bother you again." He was right.

Doc Bier's camp at Pompton Lakes, New Jersey, an hour away from New York City by car, was chosen as Louis's training site for the Carnera bout. It would be Louis's retreat for many future fights and would come to be known as his lucky camp. But at the time rumblings were heard. Neighbors called Doc Bier and warned him against opening his camp to Louis and his retinue. "We don't want niggers around here," one caller warned. The issue was raised in the newspapers. Doc Bier, a physician, stood fast. "I've rented the place and they'll be there," he said firmly. Years later, long after Louis's reign, the community of Pompton Lakes ran a dinner in his honor. The high point of the evening was the presentation to Louis of a plaque extolling him for the prestige and reflected glory he had brought to the community.

From the start, Louis was happy at Doc Bier's place. Amiability was pervasive. And the food was good. Bill Bottoms cooked thick steaks for dinner, and the entire staff, including the sparring partners, sat around a large table in the dining room of an ancient frame house and attacked the fare.

The sparring partners retained by Blackburn were taller and heavier than Louis. "You're fighting a big man in that Carnera fellow," Blackburn told Louis. "You got to hit a big man in training to get the feel of it."

Louis worked hard. He knew that his first fight in New York marked a major turning in the road. Certainly, the activity around the camp was an indication of the importance of the bout. Large crowds came out from Harlem to see his workouts in an outdoor ring pitched a hundred or so feet from a clear-water lake. Indeed, the congregation there each Sunday of his training course might have been expecting a Fourth of July picnic or a Mardi Gras parade. Hawkers sold refreshments—hot dogs, candy, soda pop. Souvenir hats and pennants were peddled. Whenever Louis landed an especially solid punch on the flabby black torso of a huge sparring partner, the brightly clad crowd howled. They shouted encouragement to Louis. He went about his business, never altering the expression on his face, unresponsive but happy.

There was stern competition among the news photographers for pictures of Louis. They had him climbing trees and fishing in the lake. They posed him devouring a steak and resting in a rocking chair on the front porch of the old house. One afternoon a photographer asked Louis to stand in front of his camera while eating a huge slice of watermelon. Louis refused. He knew a stereotype when he saw one. "No picture," he insisted. "Why not?" the cameraman asked indignantly. "Because I don't like watermelon," Louis said, stalking back into the house.

When he had concluded his training grind, Louis was a coiled spring tightened and retightened by the long

weeks of exercise. Once he was in the stadium, he un-
wound quickly. He walked out of his dressing room led by
Blackburn and Black and surrounded by a police guard.
He was rather startled by the huge crowd in the arena—
more than 62,000 persons. He didn't know it then, but
they had paid a total of $328,655 for their tickets. Later,
remembering, he said, "This was the best night in all of
my fighting. If you was ever a raggedy kid and you come
to something like that night, you'd know. I don't thrill to
things like other people. I only feel good. I felt the best
that night."

In the ring, Blackburn whispered instructions to
Louis. "Go out and hit him in the belly," the trainer said.
"His hands gonna come down. Then you go for his head."
Blackburn was right. By the fourth round, the Italian was
having difficulty coping with Louis. They went into a
clinch and Carnera attempted to bully Louis by picking
him up bodily. Louis proved stronger. He lifted Carnera
and swung him around. Carnera gasped in awe. Louis
smashed a right to the jaw. It caught Carnera with his
mouth open. His eyes went glassy. "I got him," Louis
thought. The end came in the sixth round. Louis landed
smashing punches to the head and Carnera went down.
Referee Arthur Donovan—he was to officiate in many of
Louis's bouts thereafter—picked up the count. Carnera
haunched over on both knees, listening. He came erect.
Louis threw combinations of punches to the head and
Carnera toppled again. The referee stopped the fight.
When the payoff came, Louis's purse was $60,000. He had
been a professional for only ten months.

Louis went back to Chicago and took some time off

from boxing. He went dancing with Marva and sat around with friends. To break up the routine, Louis took Marva to Detroit to visit in his mother's new house. But Louis's romantic interlude did not last too long. He was matched with King Levinsky at Comiskey Park in Chicago and he had to go back to the training camp. It was not much of a fight. Levinsky was apprehensive in the dressing room and Mike Jacobs, fearing the worst, ordered the bout to go on half an hour before its scheduled start.

"Get the fighters into the ring," the promoter screamed.

"Why? It's too early," a boxing commission official insisted.

"It's gonna rain," Jacobs said.

The official looked up. The stars shone brightly in a cloudless, moonlit sky.

Levinsky went into the ring to encounter Louis. The grim prospect of disaster held him in sway. He moved on stiff legs. Louis hit him quickly with a smashing right hand to the jaw. He responded with his own right fist, but Louis moved inside the arc of the swing. Then, countering, Louis caught Levinsky with a straight right. Levinsky toppled. Somehow he managed to rise from the canvas. Louis hit him with a left hook to the head. Levinsky went down and the fight was over. It had lasted two minutes and twenty-one seconds. For winning his twenty-fourth fight in succession, Louis was paid $53,000.

The aroma of money was in the air. Its scent filled the nostrils of Jacobs and Roxborough and Black. Together, they decided that there would be no respite for Louis. Twelve days before Louis had knocked out Carnera, Max

Baer had unexpectedly lost the world heavyweight championship to James J. Braddock on a decision in fifteen rounds. Baer's defeat had been a humiliating one. Braddock had outboxed him completely, jabbing and circling, pushing his sodden left glove against the handsome face of his victim. Baer, sadly out of condition, could not respond with his own powerful right-hand punch. The public was startled by the outcome, but nobody could believe that Baer was through as a fighter. Jacobs sensed this and decided that Baer would be Louis's next opponent. "It'll draw a million," he told Roxborough and Black.

"Joe wants to get married," Roxborough said.

"That'll wait," Jacobs said. "Where is he?"

"In Detroit," Roxborough replied.

Joe had been enjoying himself at home. Marva spent some time in Detroit, and he saw a lot of her. Afternoons, he would go out to Navin Field to watch the Detroit Tigers play. He would sit with friends in a box behind home plate and eat ice cream cones and laugh loudly when the Tigers clawed the enemy. The days were bright, and, all told, the future loomed even brighter.

When it came time to begin training for the bout with Baer, Louis went back to Pompton Lakes. He trained earnestly, methodically, though he was preparing himself for a fight with a man he could not regard too highly as a boxer. Louis had been present at Madison Square Garden Bowl, an outdoor arena in Long Island City, when Braddock had taken the title from Baer. Sitting at ringside with Roxborough, he said, "Ain't nobody gonna tell me these are the two best fighters in the world." The newspapers picked up the quotation. Baer read this and, while training at Speculator, New York, reflected on the meaning of Louis's contempt for his ability as a fighter. Mostly, Baer had never taken boxing seriously; but now, faced with the prospect of going in against Louis, he earnestly set himself to the task of attaining fighting form. When reporters visited him in camp, he spoke boldly of his impending triumph. At Pompton Lakes, Louis was as laconic as usual, outwardly unconcerned, inwardly eager for September 24 to arrive because it was also the date set for his wedding.

Louis's display of unconcern assumed a new form when Baer was late for the weigh-in scheduled for noon on the day of the fight. Instead of fretting, he nonchalantly read a newspaper. When Baer finally swaggered into the weigh-in room, he tried to upset Louis with absurdly pretentious quips. Louis ignored him. Baer, suddenly reflective, found new cause for alarm in his opponent's calmness.

That evening, two hours before the fight, Louis slipped a four-carat diamond ring on Marva's fourth finger and heard her brother, Reverend Trotter, affirm their matrimony. Then, leaving her, he rode behind a siren-screaming police escort to Yankee Stadium.

When the fight was about to begin, Blackburn told Louis, "Box him. Just stick and move, and hit him when he tries to throw his right. That'll stop him." And that's the way it was. Baer represented only a meager threat to Louis, who punished his opponent severely. In the fourth round, Baer went to the canvas under a two-handed attack and stayed there. He took the count shaking his head from side to side, probably pondering the futility of trying to stand off so devastating a puncher as Louis. An immeasurable shout went up from the throats of the 88,150 persons in the ballpark. In the fifteenth row, Mrs. Marva Louis relaxed at last. It had been a busy day for her and her husband. Not only had he gained a bride and won a fight, but he had earned $240,000 from the gross receipts of $1,000,832. Louis had brought the million-dollar gate back to boxing. In Harlem and in the other black ghettos all over America there was jubilation. Negroes ran through the streets cheering their new hero. In their exultation they found a strange new hope that somehow everything would get better for everybody among them. The next morning life was no better.

8

It was just before Christmas. Louis always spent the holiday with his wife and her mother in their Los Angeles apartment. He was not sentimentally drawn to the occasion, but he realized it meant a great deal to Martha. He was frequently capable of acts of concession, and this was one of them. But this Christmas was going to be different.

Louis phoned from New York. Martha Louis detected tension in his voice. "I'm not coming home," he said. "You come to New York."

"Listen, I've got an eighty-year-old mother and I'm not leaving her alone," Martha screamed. "And what the hell am I going to do sitting in a hotel room in New York on Christmas Eve?"

"Aw, Martha," he said. "It's no sense my coming back there. I got something to do here next week. It's a long trip if I come home and then have to come back to New York."

"You do what you please, I'm staying here," Mrs. Louis said firmly. She spent Christmas with her mother.

Often, when she is pondering the riddle of her husband's illness, Martha Louis remembers that Christmas. Was that the first sign? She finds it a hazy resolution to a profound question.

"Maybe that was it," she told an acquaintance recently, "or maybe it could have been when Joe started to tell me he'd be arriving on one plane and I'd rush out to the airport and he wouldn't be on that plane at all. He wouldn't even arrive on another plane. He'd go to another city. That happened a lot. It became a pattern of his operation. It started me to thinking."

There was another meaningful development. Martha had gone to New York to join Joe. She was accompanied by his daughter, Jacqueline. As usual, they found Joe in a suite at the Park Sheraton Hotel. Louis left the hotel alone one evening and stayed out all night. In the morning, Martha began a search for him. She called friends. They hadn't seen Joe. Visits to some of his haunts proved fruitless. The next night, when he still hadn't returned to their suite, Martha was too tense to sleep. Fretful and frustrated, she paced the floor and thought about calling the police. She rejected the notion. It might lead to publicity in the newspapers.

All the next morning, together with Jacqueline, she was absorbed in speculation about Louis's whereabouts. In these, she found no gratification. Then, toward noon, the door to the suite opened. Louis entered quietly. He was in disarray, his clothes disheveled, his sparse hair uncombed.

"Where the hell have you been?" Martha shouted. "Joe, what happened to you?"

He tried to speak, but the words came in a faltering mumble. She asked, "Joe, you been in some sort of trouble?"

He found his tongue. "I was in this place, and the police raided it."

"Didn't you tell them who you were?"

"They put all the others in one cell. They gave me a special cell."

"I don't believe you," Martha insisted. "Mean to tell me Joe Louis gets arrested and it doesn't get into the newspapers. Who you kidding?"

"That's what happened."

Aware of her dilemma, she did not press the matter any further. Her husband's explanation was either irrational or untrue. Suddenly, he was composed. "I'm sleepy," he said. "Gonna try to sleep." He chose one of the two bedrooms flanking the living room. Without removing his clothes, he dropped on the bed and muttered, "They better not start shooting the gas in here now." He got up, went to a table, and got two phone books. Then, picking up a pillow from the bed, he inserted the phone books into the pillowcase. He lay down on the bed and placed the weighted pillow over his head. "That gas ain't gonna get me now," he murmured. Somehow, he slept.

9

After their marriage, Joe and Marva shared their new six-room apartment on South Michigan Avenue in Chicago for only a few weeks before he was called back to New York. Promoter Jacobs was not committed to romance. He and his 20th Century Sporting Club could make money only when Louis was in the ring. So he hastily arranged for Joe to fight a bulky Basque named Paolino Uzcudun in Madison Square Garden.

Louis trained rigorously at Pompton Lakes, and when he climbed into the ring for the fight itself, he was in splendid condition. His movements were quick and graceful, even in the matter of just stepping through the ropes, and when he came walking down the aisle, his intensely

noble face masking confidence, the crowd rose and
cheered him. It would always be this way: his mere appearance causing a great shout to rise in the arena, to swell
when the robe draping his deeply muscled shoulders
would be removed to disclose his magnificent coffee-col-
ored torso. Even before he became champion, he looked
like one and carried himself like one. It was a quality he
would never lose.

Uzcudun fought in a crouch. He held his gloves up
in front of his face, peering between them at Louis, duck-
ing under punches, straining to neutralize his tormentor's
power by depriving him of an open target. For three
rounds, Louis was perplexed. In the fourth, Uzcudun
committed a palpable blunder. He spread his gloved hands
apart about six inches to see Louis clearly. A right-hand
blow breached the gap, landing on the Basque's face with
such force, it drove two of his teeth through his lower lip.
Blood spurted. The referee stopped the fight. "I never
threw a better punch," Louis said. To which Blackburn
added, "Or a harder one."

From a ringside seat, Max Schmeling watched the
fight closely. Once the heavyweight champion, the German fighter was now in the waning days of his career. He
had always been a thoughtful student of boxing, and the
opportunity to see Louis in action was a laboratory session
for him. "I seez somezing," he told the reporters. Just
what it was he saw he would not say, but the sportswriters
took him seriously because of his acknowledged understanding of boxing. In addition, he was going to be Louis's
next major opponent, and anything he said in regard to his
rival was of instant importance. Another important decla-
ration was made—this one by Louis's directorate. For the

first time since his advent on New York, he would not train at Pompton Lakes.

Approximately sixty miles south of Pompton Lakes, in Jersey pine country, is Lakewood, a town made famous by John D. Rockefeller. Newspaper pictures and newsreels often portrayed him playing golf on his estate there. Before the popularity of Florida as a resort, New Yorkers on vacation flocked to Lakewood because its mean temperature in winter was several degrees higher than New York's. There were many hotels in the town and its environs, and it was one of these hotels, the Stanley, that was chosen as Louis's training camp for the fight with Schmeling.

"I think a change from Pompton Lakes will do Joe good," Roxborough said, though there was cause later to doubt the wisdom of the move. Things did not evolve as Roxborough had prophesied.

For one thing, Schmeling was regarded as a relatively old man. Six years had passed since he had lost the heavyweight title to Jack Sharkey. He was, at thirty-one years of age, nine years older than Louis. Bookmakers quickly made Louis a 10-to-1 favorite. In Lakewood, unbridled confidence reigned. It resulted in a lapse in discipline. Marva came to the Stanley Hotel and spent a few days with her husband. A carnival atmosphere pervaded the place. In the hotel, somebody had set up an electrically wired chair in which newcomers to the camp were seated. When the current was turned on, the one occupying the chair received a mild electric shock and leaped in panic. Louis howled. But even this relaxation from serious training was not a determining factor in Louis's condition. Golf

was. Not only was he introduced to the game at Lakewood, but he went at it avidly, playing the course almost
daily with some of the newspapermen assigned to cover
his training activities.

"Chappie, that ain't good for you," Blackburn
warned the fighter. "It's okay," Louis said. "I walk. That's
good for my legs."

"The timing's different. And them muscles you use in
golf, they ain't the same ones you use hitting a man.
Besides, being out in the sun don't do you no good. You'll
be dried out."

In the training ring, Louis proceeded to knock down
his sparring partners. So apprehension waned, and when
Louis and his faction broke camp on the morning of the
fight and rode to New York for the weigh-in, nobody in
his party even thought of impending defeat as they
checked into the Hotel Theresa in Harlem. That afternoon
it rained, and the fight, scheduled for Yankee Stadium,
was postponed until the next night.

There were more than 42,000 persons in the stadium
when Louis climbed through the ropes. He looked across
the ring and spotted Schmeling seated on his stool, his
black hair neatly combed, his face inscrutable, his concen-
tration unimpaired by the excitement around him. Louis
thought, "He a cool man."

The opening bell rang. Louis walked to the center of
the ring and found Schmeling waiting for him. The German's left arm was extended. His right fist was cocked at
the chest, while his chin was tucked in at his collarbone,
affording it protection from Louis's punches. For three
rounds, Louis couldn't land a solid right. He depended

[68]

almost totally on his left. A jab opened a cut under Schmeling's right eye. He ignored the trickle of blood. Louis thought, "Keep hittin' him with the left." But then, in the next round, it happened. Louis shifted to throw a left jab. Schmeling reacted sharply. He crossed Louis's left with his own right fist. It landed on Louis's chin. In a flash, another right caught Louis on the jaw. He sank to the canvas. He had never been on the floor as a professional. He heard the referee's count. It reached three. He managed to get to his feet and finish the round.

In the corner Blackburn scolded him. "I told you to watch that right," the trainer screamed. In the fifth round, Schmeling was right back with his right fist. It landed on the jaw. Louis's ears were ringing. His swollen jaw felt heavy and painful. He heard the bell ending the fifth round and dropped his hands. Another right crashed against his jaw. It sent him sprawling on the canvas. His handlers rushed in and pulled him to the corner. Referee Donovan warned Schmeling against hitting after the bell.

Subsequently, Louis said, "People put it out that I hated Schmeling for hitting me after the bell. I never hated him. We became friends. After the fight, he sent me one of those German cuckoo clocks. Ain't no reason to hate a man just because he beats you in a fight."

Louis was badly beaten. Schmeling finished him off in the twelfth round. The final punch was a right to the jaw. Louis went to the canvas slowly. Then, stretching out, he rested his head on his right glove. "When the referee counted," he said later, "it came to me faint, like somebody whispering. It didn't make no difference."

It was Louis's first defeat in twenty-eight professional

bouts. The press had built him up as a superman, and he had been proved vulnerable. Schmeling had, in fact, seen "somezing" in Louis's fight with Uzcudun. It concerned Joe's habit of dropping his left arm after throwing a jab, thus exposing himself to a right cross. The German took advantage of the discovery.

Marva had been persuaded by a woman reporter to accompany her to the fight. When Louis went down the first time, she wanted to flee, but her companion insisted that she stay. For a long time afterward she had nightmares. She would see Louis with his face swollen and his eyes closed, and Schmeling's right hand landing again and again.

10

The Louises were in Las Vegas, staying at Caesars Palace. Joe appeared distressed and Martha thought, "I wonder why? I don't mind being a fool, but I want to be an informed fool." She had learned that anything she wanted to know about her husband's covert behavior had to be uncovered by her own investigation. But she was a female and there was coupled with her devotion to investigation a sense of intuition. Something was wrong, and she was determined to find out its cause.

Her suspicion had been aroused by a phone call. When Louis got off the phone, Martha noted that he was extremely agitated. "What's the matter, Joe? You got some girl pregnant?"

"Oh, no, no," he said. "Wish I was as good a man as you give me credit for."

"Oh, come, come," Martha said. "Why don't you tell me the truth?"

Louis forced a smile. "Ain't nothing to it," he said.

Martha fought off impending anger. Composed, she made an unannounced decision to look further into the matter. As defense attorney in many criminal cases, she had learned to discount theory. She preferred facts and she knew these to be elusive—gained only through application and hard work.

Louis had to fly to New York to attend a sports dinner. "Why don't you call the Park Sheraton and get me a reservation?" he told Martha.

Martha phoned New York and asked for the suite the Louises usually occupied on the twenty-fourth floor. "We liked it because it had two phones," she explained later, "and you know I'm big on using the phone a lot."

It had been Martha's intention to join her husband in New York, but a legal matter came up that demanded her immediate attention in Los Angeles. She remained at home. So Joe was in New York alone; and when Martha phoned him, she was told that he was not in the usual suite but was staying in Room 1026 instead.

New suspicions were aroused. Martha could not wait until she could confront Joe. Instead of returning to Las Vegas, Louis flew to Oakland to attend an important sports function. Martha was in the vicinity, conferring with a client in a state penitentiary, and found it convenient to greet her husband at the airport.

"Hello, Joe," she called when she spotted Louis at the airport. "Have a good trip?"

"It was all right," Louis responded.

"You had a different room, didn't you?"

"Yeah, they knew I liked this other room," Louis said.

Martha Louis dropped the subject. She had been pursuing her inquiry along other lines and was well on her way. When she asked some of Louis's friends for their testimony in this matter, they reacted like this: "Honest, Martha, we don't know what you're talking about. Ain't nothing wrong we know about." But she made progress in another direction.

Some time later, the Louises went to Miami Beach and stayed at a hotel recently opened by the Hilton chain. Just before Valentine's Day, several greeting cards arrived for Louis. Their salutation was: "For Daddy." Moreover, the envelopes bore the number of the room in which the Louises were staying. One was signed "Marie."

"What about these?" Martha asked.

"Don't know anything about them," Louis said.

"Now look, you're talking to me. Impossible for somebody to know your room number when you got here yesterday."

"You explain it," Louis said.

"Well, let me tell you something. You would have had to be in contact with the person who knew the room number. That's all I got to say."

And that, for the moment, was where the matter rested. Soon thereafter the Louises left for New York. They registered at the Park Sheraton. Within a few days, Martha Louis had all the information she needed. It had come from one of Louis's more talkative cronies.

As she was eventually to describe it, her confrontation of Louis with the news produced anything but a sensation.

"Joe, look, you're talking to me," Martha said quietly. "For one time, tell me the truth. Not only am I your wife, I'm your friend. What about this baby that was born on December 2, 1967?"

"I ain't seen that girl but once," Louis said coldly. "She's a $50 trick. And I've never seen the baby."

"Great," Martha replied. She thought, "I'll let this much sink in. Maybe Joe will start talking about it later." He didn't, and a few days later Martha went back at him. She told him, "Look, Joe, let me make a deal with you. Since you don't know where the baby is and you've seen this woman but once, what about me talking to her?"

"Yeah, you can talk to her. Sure."

Louis said this quickly. He was not aware that Martha Louis had discovered that the woman was living in the same hotel, in Room 1026, the very one Louis had occupied when he had been in New York alone earlier.

It was Sunday morning, March 3, 1968. The Louises were lounging around in their suite. Joe said, "Martha, I think I'll go up to the Red Rooster in Harlem." She hastily suggested that she accompany him. "Don't you think I'm big enough to go by myself?" he asked. She acknowledged that he was.

"You'll probably be gone by the time I get back," Martha said. "I'm going right downstairs now to have breakfast."

"I'll wait until you get back," Louis said. "No hurry."

The picture came into focus. Louis was not going up to Harlem. What he planned to do was to take the elevator to the tenth floor and to enter Room 1026. But he did not want to be floating around the hotel while Martha was out of the suite. There was always the chance they might run into each other. He decided to wait in the suite until Martha returned from breakfast.

When she returned, Joe said, "Okay, I'm going. Be home about three." When he had not returned by four o'clock, Martha Louis was steaming. She told herself, "He must think I'm the biggest fool in the world. He's got a girl in the hotel and he's telling me he's going up to Harlem."

Martha reacted immediately. She picked up the phone and called Room 1026. A female answered. "Listen, I want to tell you one thing," Martha said forcefully. "I know Joe's down there, and I have made up my mind exactly what I'm going to do. You just tell that to Joe."

Then, hanging up, she put in another call, this one to Freddie Wilson. He had been one of Louis's sparring partners, and they had remained friends. Louis had been good to Wilson. He had kept him around as his chauffeur and, later, had obtained a job for him with the National Maritime Union in New York. They were fond of each other, and Wilson was one of Louis's confidants.

On the phone, Martha calmly informed Wilson that she knew of Louis's presence in Room 1026. "And what is more, I know all about the baby, and you can tell that to Joe," Martha said. Wilson, not usually a talkative man, was deprived even of his few words. Finally, gasping, he managed to say, "Oh, my God." That was all. When he was finished listening to Martha, he phoned Louis and told him about the call he had just received.

Back in the suite, Martha thought that Louis would react in one of two ways: either he would face her sheepishly and take the music or he would rush away somewhere. She favored the first hypothesis, but she was wrong. No sooner had her husband said good-bye to Wilson than he left the Park Sheraton and went to the airport, where he boarded a plane for Detroit. All that sleepless night she waited for him, somehow believing he would return at any moment.

The next day, Monday, March 4, 1968, was a historic one in boxing. The new Madison Square Garden was to open, and Louis had been invited to be introduced from the ring before the main event between Joe Frazier and Buster Mathis. He didn't show up. Neither did Martha. She had spent a busy day.

Remembering it, Martha remarked, "I like to face up to a situation. If you find out the truth, at least you can accept it or reject it; you know where you're going. I'm capable of coping with anything, I think, and that's the way it was when this baby situation came up."

As she sat in the living room of the suite waiting for Louis, Martha decided to call the woman in Room 1026.

"You come up here or I'll come down to you," she said on the phone. "Don't make no difference to me."

"I'll come up there," the other one said.

Before long there was a knock on the door. Martha Louis opened it.

"I'm Marie Johnson," the woman said. She motioned toward a young man who was with her. "I brought him along. I was afraid something could happen. I told him I owed you a hundred dollars and I didn't have it. He can be here while we talk."

"Come in," Martha said.

Martha's eyes measured the other woman. She was small. "Thin," Martha would say later, "with a little behind about as big as your hand. But I admired her. She had enough spunk to come and see me. I couldn't take that away from her."

"I'm going to talk frankly to you, Marie," Martha Louis said. "It was no accident on your part. What you did, going and having a baby, was no accident. And you don't even know if it's Joe's baby."

"Them things happen," Marie said.

"I'm not going to argue. What I'm concerned about is the baby."

"He's all right. Got good care for him with my family."

"I'd like to take him," Martha Louis said. "We can give him a lot of love and protection." She thought, "I know this girl's been in prostitution and in prison. That baby deserves better."

"One thing, don't get on Joe when you see him," Marie said. "He was awful jittery yesterday when he found out you knew about the baby. Just forget about everything."

"He's my husband. I'll handle him."

"He told me a lot of nice things about you," Marie said, "about how his children like you very much and you go to church. But the only thing is you don't have enough time for him."

Martha allowed herself a smile. "Poor, neglected Joe," she thought.

They talked for more than an hour. Marie, it developed, was twenty-three years of age. She was born in Steubenville, Ohio; but her family now lived in the metropolitan area of New York. She had been on her own since she was thirteen or fourteen; and at the time she met Louis, she was on parole from the women's prison at Bedford Hills, New York. Joe had been introduced to her in a Manhattan cocktail bar, where she was a waitress.

When Martha and Marie had finished their discussion, it was agreed that Martha would take the baby. And when they parted, they were friends.

Before long, the phone rang in the suite. It was Louis calling from Detroit.

"When you coming back here?" Martha asked.

"I'll be there tomorrow," Louis said, as though nothing unusual had happened. He kept his word.

11

In Detroit, sitting around his mother's house, Louis tried
to remember how it had been in the minutes and hours
after the knockout by Schmeling. His head had throbbed,
and Blackburn had applied ice packs to his eyes and his
cheeks. Then, back at the Theresa, he had looked into a
mirror. He shuddered and heard his sister Vunies say,
"Joe, your head looks like a watermelon." Nobody
laughed. Within a few days, the swelling was down. When
it was time to leave New York, Joe and Marva thought
about going home to Chicago, but they decided he would
be better off in Detroit, where they could spend time with
his mother. Mrs. Barrow treated her son as though he

were a youngster again, cooking the food he liked, speaking words of consolation, as if he had been in a fight with the kid next door and had come home crying. His spirit was nourished, and before long he was moving around town.

Newspapermen prodded him. Had he, a black hero, let his people down by losing to Schmeling? He had no coherent view of society, but he sensed that mere victory or defeat in the ring would not diminish racial discrimination and the exploitation of black Americans. "When I lost," he said, "I didn't hurt my people. There are just as many Negro doctors, lawyers, and politicians as before I was whupped. And none of the poor ain't suddenly rich either."

In Detroit he played some golf. He rode horses and took in shows. He was enjoying himself away from boxing, but there was a nagging compulsion to prove that the knockout by Schmeling had not finished him as a fighter. He went back to Chicago, and nothing he did in the way of recreation seemed to please him. Then the waiting ended. Mike Jacobs arranged a match at Yankee Stadium with Jack Sharkey. Jacobs was smart. Sharkey had beaten Schmeling for the championship four years before; and though Sharkey had surprisingly lost it to Carnera and even though time had deprived him of his skills, he still retained status. Lately, he had engaged in a comeback with only moderate success—in Jacobs's promotional view it was enough to qualify him as the perfect foil for Louis's reentry into the arena.

Louis went back to Pompton Lakes to train. The folly of Lakewood was behind him. Newspapermen asked him whether the defeat by Schmeling had taken the heart out of him. His responses, monosyllabic though they were, committed him to atoning for that defeat. Blackburn worked him hard. He stressed defense against the right-hand punch. And he ordered Louis's sparring partners to throw their rights at will. "That's what Sharkey's gonna try on Joe," Blackburn said. And he told Joe, "Lead to that man, and he'll try to hit you with rights, the way Schmeling did. Watch for it."

Louis followed Blackburn's orders. In the first round, he hit Sharkey with solid jabs to the head. Sharkey moved inside a jab and threw a hard right. Louis blocked it. Then, responding with his own right fist, he hurt Sharkey just before the bell. It took Louis two more rounds to finish the job. The crushing blow was a right to the jaw. Sharkey wavered and then fell forward. He had been bold in his endeavor, but Louis was altogether too destructive for him. Louis had scored his twenty-fourth knockout. In the dressing room later, Blackburn told newspapermen, "Joe's mad at Schmeling, but Sharkey paid for it."

Little more than a month later, Louis was back in the ring again, this time in Philadelphia. He flattened Al Ettore in five rounds. Within seventeen days, he fought Jorge Brescia, an Argentine, at the Hippodrome in New York. The fight lasted three rounds. The busy schedule was purposefully arranged. Not only did it keep Louis's mind on boxing, but it rehabilitated his public image. Once again he was the Brown Bomber. He went around the country on an exhibition tour and knocked out four opponents in South Bend and New Orleans. In Cleveland, in a bout scheduled for ten rounds, he disposed of Eddie Simms in the first round. He hit Simms so hard the fallen victim looked up at the referee Arthur Donovan, and said, "Let's go on the roof. I want to get some fresh air."

Early the next year, 1937, Louis went into the Madison Square Garden ring with Bob Pastor. Bookmakers rated Louis at odds of 2-to-1 to score a knockout; but they had not considered in their calculations the wily Jimmy Johnston, who handled Pastor's affairs though he was the boxing promoter in the Garden and, thus, officially ineligible to manage a fighter. Johnston had never forgotten that Roxborough and Black had turned him down when he had come to them in quest of exclusive promotional control of Louis, a right granted instead to Jacobs and the 20th Century Sporting Club. Johnston mapped Pastor's strategy. He ordered his fighter to keep on the move. "Louis can't hit you if you don't stand still," he said. So Pastor ran for ten rounds, and Louis could not land a knockout punch. "Pin him in a corner," Blackburn pleaded with Louis. But Pastor was elusive, though hardly aggressive; and when the fight was over, Louis's hand was raised in victory. He had won a decision, but he had failed to knock out Pastor. "I felt bad about that fight," Louis remembers. Johnston gloated. Less than a month later, Louis fought Natie Brown in Kansas City. It was an interesting match. Brown, by going the distance, had spoiled Louis's "coming out" party in Detroit the night the New York sportswriters had first seen him in action. Then Louis had failed to knock him out. In Kansas City he was disposed of in four rounds.

What followed in Louis's career was a fine specimen of boxing intrigue. Mike Jacobs was the arch plotter.

Aware that Braddock, the heavyweight champion, was under exclusive contract to Madison Square Garden, he set in motion a plot to deprive the Garden of Braddock's services for a title fight with Schmeling, scheduled for the Madison Square Garden Bowl in Long Island City on June 3, 1937.

Jacobs had tried earlier to persuade Schmeling to give the Brown Bomber a return match. Schmeling refused. Instead, he signed to fight Braddock under the Garden's auspices and returned to Nazi Germany comforted by the notion that he would soon bring the heavyweight championship of the world back to the fatherland. It was the worst of times. Adolf Hitler's vile philosophy of racial superiority was national policy. In the adroit hands of Hitler's propaganda chief Paul Joseph Goebbels, it assumed many wicked forms. Goebbels now proceeded to use Schmeling as a symbol of what the Nazis called Aryan supremacy. A dwarfish man with a crippled foot, a neurotic personality, and an agile mind, Goebbels put words in Schmeling's mouth. "The black man will always be afraid of me," the German press quoted Schmeling as saying. "He is inferior." Schmeling was in no position in Nazi Germany to deny the statement. It cost him any sympathy he might have gained in America as a result of Jacobs's conspiracy to deprive him of a shot at Braddock's title. Louis, characteristically passive, simply brushed it off. Publicly, he feigned anger; privately, he respected Schmeling as a prizefighter and said so to his cronies.

Joe Gould was Braddock's manager. A small, sharp-nosed little man, he had been insignificant in the fight business until Braddock's unexpected ascension to the heavyweight throne. He was conspiratorial by nature and quickly involved himself in Jacobs's scheme. In exchange for ten percent of Jacobs's *net* profits from heavyweight championship bouts for the next ten years, he signed a contract for Braddock to defend the title against Louis in Chicago's Comiskey Park on June 22, 1937. Years later, he would sue Jacobs for his and Braddock's share of the profits; but at that time, in 1937, he was the promoter's associate.

Madison Square Garden brought suit in federal court to enjoin Braddock, insisting that he was obligated by contract to defend his title only under auspices of the Garden. Jacobs did not worry. Sol Strauss, his hard-of-hearing Pickwickian lawyer, read the contract between Braddock and the Garden and reached the conclusion that it was invalid in equity because it tied Braddock to the Garden without imposing any obligations on the Garden itself. In Newark, New Jersey, Judge Guy L. Fake handed down a decision against the Garden. Schmeling continued to train for the fight with Braddock. The New York State Athletic Commission even went through the pretense of holding a weighing-in ceremony. But on the night of June 3, Madison Square Garden Bowl was cloaked in darkness. The Braddock–Schmeling match had become a "phantom fight."

Louis, meanwhile, had begun preparations for the championship event. He went to Stevensville, Michigan, and relaxed for more than a fortnight. "He's buildin' up energy," Blackburn explained. When Louis left Stevensville for Kenosha, Wisconsin, he was ready for earnest training. In Kenosha, on the shore of Lake Michigan, he lived in a large brick house. Breezes off the lake cooled the house, and it was a pleasant place for sleeping. In all, it was a genial camp, though a new element was on the scene. Harry Lenny, a veteran trainer of fighters, had been brought into the camp to demonstrate to Louis how to defend himself against right-hand punches. Blackburn did not protest. "If it helps Chappie become champ, it's good," he said.

A rigorous training schedule was invoked. Louis, who would spar on alternate days, ran ten miles on the road each morning. Up at five o'clock, he would lead Blackburn and Carl Nelson, a Chicago detective who was his bodyguard, into the half-light of morning. Then, with them trailing him in a car, he would measure ten miles over the undulating countryside. Returning to camp, he would sleep until ten o'clock. Breakfast consisted of orange juice, prunes, and lamb chops or liver. Then, after several hours of relaxation, he would either do limbering-up exercises or take on his sparring partners. He was relentless in target practice, hitting his sparmates as hard and as often as he could. By the time he got to Bill Bottoms's fare again, he was starved. Meat, fish, vegetables, ice cream were avidly consumed. Louis was in camp on his twenty-third birthday, May 13, 1937. Bottoms baked a cake for him. Everybody wished him a happy birthday; and when he turned in as usual at nine o'clock, he was the most gratified man in all of Wisconsin.

No concern ruffled him when he climbed into the ring at Comiskey Park. He wore his lucky blue bathrobe with red trim and the usual mask of majestic impassivity. He was not yet the king of the heavyweights, but his bearing, so regal in all outward appearances, marked him as the inevitable conqueror. All he had to do was to lay his heavy hand on the enemy to achieve his lofty purpose. It was that simple an equation.

Blackburn whispered to him, "Chappie, this is it. You come home a champ tonight." Then the bell rang.

Louis walked toward Braddock. He knew the man well. Braddock had won the title from Baer two years before and had not engaged in a bout since then. And when surprisingly he had won it, he had been called the "Cinderella Man" because he had come off the home relief rolls to achieve his greatest triumph. But now, in the ring with the young Louis, he suddenly appeared older, slow, almost slothful. He wasn't. He threw the first heavy punch of the night, a right. Louis moved inside it and thought, "That's it. That right. I got to watch it."

Louis tried his jab. The left fist found Braddock's face, but he countered with a right. Again, Louis stepped inside the punch. Now, moving in, Louis responded with his own right. Almost instantly, Braddock smashed a hard right to the jaw. It took Louis off his feet. He thought, "It don't hurt." He jumped up instantly.

In the corner, between rounds, Blackburn screamed, "Why didn't you take a nine-count? You can't get up so fast that nobody in the place didn't see you was down. And keep jabbin'."

Emboldened by the knockdown, Braddock came forth strongly at the start of the next round. He threw a flurry of punches. Some landed, some were warded off by Louis's gloves. Braddock pressed the attack, and Louis countered with hard rights. Two punches bounced off

Braddock's jaw, and he replied with a right against Louis's chest. In return he took some heavy blows to the head. Now, pained, Braddock began throwing punches wildly. Louis retained his poise and punished the old champion.

In the third round Louis caught Braddock with several stiff jabs. One of them opened a cut over Braddock's upper lip. Blood smeared his chin. He appeared near collapse, his vision blurred beneath the hot white overhead lights, his body aching, his spirit calling upon resources only brave men have at their command. They carried him into the eighth round.

Now, deprived of all but courage, Braddock was an open target. He was pawing the air with his gloves, straining instinctively to reach Louis, never quite getting there. Instead, wobbly, he moved into a right-hand smash to the jaw. Louis put everything behind it. It seemed to split Braddock's face in two. He fell forward, then found himself sitting on the canvas, his right hand supporting him, his left arm hanging limply. The referee, Tommy Thomas, counted him out.

The end was not a complicated thing for the 45,000 persons in Comiskey Park to comprehend. And the consequences were just as obvious. Joe Louis was the world heavyweight champion, and, yet, nothing had changed, either inside the arena or outside. On Chicago's South Side black Americans came charging out of their houses, shouting jubilantly, cheering their hero. But he was not really theirs; he belonged to everybody. It was an emotional night, yet it moved Louis to say only, "I don't want nobody to call me champ till I beat that Schmeling."

12

When Marie Johnson's baby was four months old, Martha took him to Detroit for a visit. He was known as Joseph Louis, but everybody called him "Jo-Jo." The visit was brief and the baby was returned to his mother. A month later, however, Martha again took the child, this time to Los Angeles. Jo-Jo has been with her ever since. Louis, who was beginning to display precipitate changes of mood, was invariably kind in his treatment of Jo-Jo. Once, asked about the child, he said, "He a good kid. I want to keep him. Don't matter none. When you're laying around with a whore, who knows who the father is?" He said this dispassionately, conveying neither a sense of shock nor a feeling of remorse. It was, to him, a simple fact of life in his time.

During his days as a fighter and later, fastidiousness had been one of his traits. He paid considerable attention to his clothes and hygiene. Even in training, he had been immaculate. His dressing room at camp was brightly clean, and he wore newly laundered boxing garb each training day. But now, in 1968, there developed an alteration in his attitude toward clothes.

Martha said, "This is one of the things that worried me. He used to change his clothes twice a day. Everything had to be just so, underwear and everything. And he'd shower twice a day, especially when he was playing golf. But then I noticed that he wasn't paying attention to such things. When we'd go out to my mother—she lives five blocks from us in Los Angeles now, but she used to live in Pasadena—I'd say, 'Joe, why don't you put on a different shirt? Why don't you change?' He'd say, 'Oh, this is all right, nothing wrong with it.' You know, his trousers would be baggy, with the crease out of them or grease spots on them. And off he'd go."

During this period, they visited Chicago together; and when Martha left for Los Angeles alone, a significant incident happened.

"You take my golf clubs home with you," Joe said. "I won't need them."

"But you always keep them with you."

"Won't need them," Joe said petulantly.

So Martha took the clubs with her. Louis did not touch them for five months, an unusually long gap in his devotion to the game. "Joe lost interest in golf and lost interest in everything else," Martha said.

In the comfortless course of his driftings, Louis kept Martha in the dark about his travel arrangements. He would tell her that he would take a specific flight to Chicago and then turn up in Detroit on another plane. It happened frequently. Martha knew no explanation, nor did Louis offer one, not immediately anyway. If there was a change in his plans, he simply would not tell her, nor would any of his cronies know about it.

"When he'd be home, he'd stay in bed all day," Martha said. "I'd say, 'Joe, you have a date for golf.' He'd say, 'Call that guy and tell him I'm not playing.' It wasn't like Joe. Before this, golf seemed to be the most important thing in his life. If you ask me, I'd tell you it was more important than women. Come to think of it, women weren't that important either. I think Joe's really a man's man. He likes to be around with his friends. I think he puts friends ahead of family.".

The family was together in Los Angeles—Joe, Martha, and Martha's mother. Louis pulled out a pack of cigarettes, put a match to one, and began to smoke.

"Joe, what you doing smoking?" Martha's mother asked. "Everybody else is trying to stop smoking and talking about cancer."

Louis kept on puffing. Martha thought, "How about that? This man having had the reputation that he's had all these years for clean living just picking up and smoking?" Measured against the future, the incident was a mere thunderstorm preceding the long, dark, gyrating funnel of a tornado.

13

Louis was the world heavyweight champion; but, of course, the defeat by Schmeling still bothered him. Although he accepted his royal status with the straightest of faces, he reflected often on the need to reestablish his invincibility by beating Schmeling. Not that he spent his days and nights concerning himself with the matter. By then, he had become a practiced hand in pleasure and indulged himself in it with increasing frequency. But time was the enemy of his indulgence. He could not play around and retain his fighting shape, not with the busy schedule arranged for him by his faction. Within nine months of his defeat of Braddock, he defended the title three times. Tommy Farr, a sturdy Welshman, went fifteen rounds with him. Then, moving into 1938, he knocked out Nathan Mann and Harry Thomas. Without exception, sports fanatics awaited the second meeting of Louis and Schmeling. But the fight held more than just the promise of a mere sports spectacle.

It was the period in history of Neville Chamberlain and his unhappy, fruitless quest for "peace in our time." Hitler was on the prowl in Europe, and little more than a year later Warsaw would die in flames. The world, changing, was heading for a holocaust; and against this background of disorder, America was being torn by partisanship. Deluded Americans of German ancestry organized the German-American Bund. Parading in Nazi-like uniforms, they went into encampments and wielded weapons on rifle ranges. They held dirty hands with the Ku Klux Klan. America, torn emotionally by fear, found a meaning in the fight that transcended its actual value and rendered Schmeling a symbol of Nazi arrogance. Even before official contracts for the fight were signed, the Anti-Nazi League to Champion Human Rights threatened to throw a picket line around promoter Jacobs's offices. President Franklin D. Roosevelt got into the act inadvertently.

Earlier in 1938, Louis had been invited to attend the Negro Elks convention in Washington. He was awarded an honorary life-membership gold card in the Elks and rode in the marshal's car in the organization's parade. Later, Roosevelt asked him to come to the White House, and a presidential limousine was sent around to Louis's hotel to pick him up. Louis, accompanied by Mal Frazier, a friend, was escorted into the President's office, where he

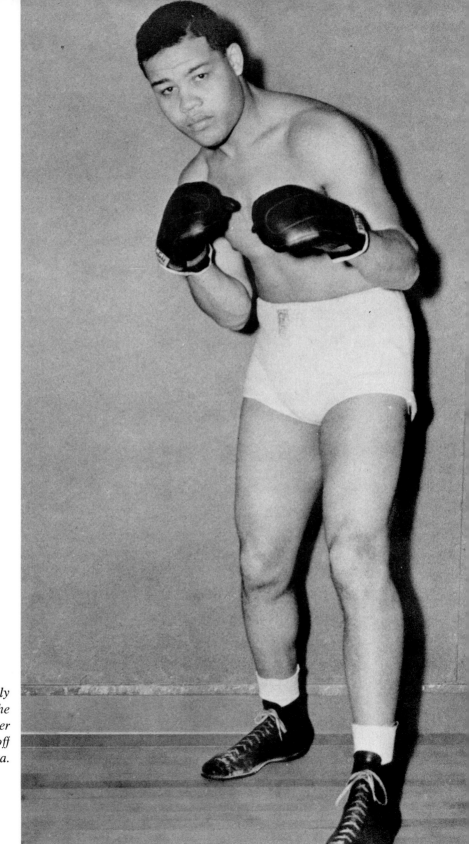

In an early publicity shot, the Brown Bomber squares off at the camera.

Upon his arrival in New York in 1935 (lower left), *with Julian Black,
on his left, and John Roxborough, Joe Louis is paid a cheering
tribute by redcaps (above). An unmarked Louis preens (below
right)* directly after his knockout victory over Primo Carnera.
Louis, early in his career, with trainer Jack Blackburn (facing page).

LOUIS

Joe (above) *surrounded by fans in Harlem, shortly after his defeat of Primo Carnera. Boxing promoter Mike Jacobs chats with Louis* (below).

Joe (facing page) *spars at his Lakewood, New Jersey, training camp in preparation for his first fight with Max Schmeling.*

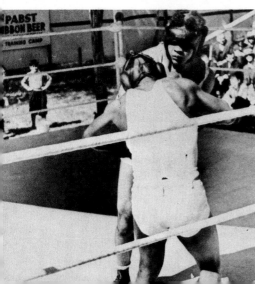

Following his victory over Max Schmeling (above left), *Louis shares a light moment with his wife Marva and tap dancer Bill Robinson. The champ and Marva are shown (above right) arriving in Chicago in 1939. Louis assumes a new role (below), refereeing an amateur bout in Madison Square Garden. Back in training (below right), manager Roxborough restrains the hungry champ, but at right....*

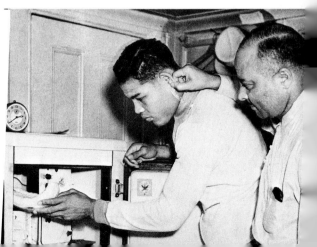

A bearded Louis walks in the rain at his Pompton Lakes training camp (above left). With his first wife Marva (above right), Louis attends a horse show. Joe takes an equestrian break from training (below).

found Roosevelt seated at his desk. The world heavy-weight champion was greeted warmly. After a few minutes, Roosevelt said to Louis, "Lean over, Joe, so I can feel your muscles." Louis did. Roosevelt said, "Joe, we need muscles like yours to beat Germany." That is all that was said. But when the story was repeated, it came out to be something else: that the President had said, "Joe, beat Schmeling to prove we can beat the Germans."

Louis prepared carefully for the fight with Schmeling. He went to Stevensville, Michigan, and rested. In mid-May, he switched to Lafayetteville, New York, where he ran a few miles each morning and spent some time chopping wood. Then, ready for heavy sparring drills, he went to Pompton Lakes. His major sparring partners were George Nicholson and Willie Reddish. They pressed him to the limit in the practice ring. His sparring sessions on Saturdays and Sundays attracted huge throngs, perhaps as many as 5,000 persons at times. They cluttered the camp and bought soda pop and souvenirs avidly. He besought fighting form just as greedily. Newspapermen repeatedly reminded him that in Schmeling he would be confronting a dangerous opponent. Louis responded, "Schmeling's got to be good. He knocked me out."

Up at Speculator, New York, Schmeling trained in quieter Adirondacks surroundings. Max Machon was his trainer and confidant. Sharp-nosed, slight of build, Machon represented to the innocent American a typical Nazi —his abrasiveness was expressed in his speech mannerism, which was sharp and edged with sarcasm. One day, a newspaperman named Harry Sperber—himself a refugee from Nazi Germany—put out a story in a German-language newspaper that he had spotted a Nazi uniform in Machon's closet in the house in which Schmeling's entourage lived, down the road from a lake-side inn called Osborne's Hotel. The story was picked up by other sports journalists. It served further to incite hatred for Schmeling. What was just a prize fight had become a national cause.

In Schmeling's camp, Arno Helmers, an official Nazi broadcaster, sent stories back to Germany that represented New York's Governor Herbert Lehman as a conspirator in a plot to ensure Schmeling's defeat. How this was to be achieved was never detailed. The basis for the story was that the governor was a Jew. When Nazi reaction to Helmer's hoax was reported back to America, it added fuel to an already raging fire. In the reflection of the blaze, promoter Jacobs's blue eyes grew wider and wider. Ringside tickets, priced at $40 each, were selling even beyond his wildest dreams of avarice. Then, into the propaganda mill was dropped another external matter that added to America's misguided evaluation of the fight. Eighteen American citizens were indicted as spies for Nazi Germany.

At Pompton Lakes, Louis was relaxed. He was concerned only with victory, which he wanted to achieve without recourse to personal hatred. Winning was important, but what it had to do with national or racial superiority was not Louis's basic concern. Two men were going to fight, each straining for victory, neither truly concerned with national aspirations because he was not a political animal. And both were trained to the edge of perfection, Louis at 198¾ pounds, Schmeling at 193 pounds.

[94]

Louis remembers what it was like driving to the stadium that night, June 22, 1938. "There were cops wherever you looked," he recalls. "When we got to the stadium, you could hardly get in. Them bluecoats were everywhere. Going up, we didn't laugh much. Nobody made jokes. It was an important fight."

The crowd inside Yankee Stadium attested to this. More than 70,000 persons were there; and, later, when Jacobs counted the receipts, he found $1,015,012 in his treasury. Surreptitiously, he had cleaned up a fortune by scalping tickets. Some ringsiders had paid as much as $200 each for seats. Even the working-press section had provided a source of "black market" revenue for Jacobs. Normally restricted to accredited reporters, it contained in its crowded confines Jacobs's "personal" customers. They had paid him as much as $500 each to be so close to the ring as actually to see the tensing muscles of the fighters.

Louis took a long warm-up in the dressing room, shadow boxing to bring his magnificent body to a light sweat. And then he was summoned to battle. He came out of the dressing room, through a dugout and across the field, led by Blackburn and Black and protected by a squad of policemen. He went up into the ring, and the crowd saw him, saw the same blue and red bathrobe he had worn the first time he had fought Schmeling. An immeasurable shout filled the ballpark, the kind the stadium had first heard years ago when Babe Ruth rode one into the stands during a World Series. Schmeling came next, draped in an old gray bathrobe. Early boos gave way to faint cheers. A tentative smile edged Schmeling's thin lips. Now it was suddenly quiet, and in the press rows broadcasters could be heard describing the scene. Louis, paying attention only to his handlers, began hitting the air with punches, keeping warm for the battle ahead.

The prefight conference at midring was brief. Referee Donovan issued the usual instruction. In living rooms and kitchens throughout the country, millions moved closer to their radios. In Germany, where it was three o'clock in the morning, Arno Helmers's gruff voice was being heard on the national network of the Third Reich.

The bell sounded, and a hush fell over the stadium. One never fortunate enough to have seen Louis in action in the ring can never know how it was at the start of one of his fights: the shuffling movement of creeping death, the fists in perfect position, the left extended, the right poised, and the witnesses' hearts pumping just a little faster than usual. And that is how it was against Schmeling. Louis eyed him for seemingly long seconds; and Schmeling, abjuring an opening gesture, backed away. Then the champion pushed two jabs into Schmeling's face. The German took several backward steps, and Louis leaped in. Schmeling caught him with a punch to the head, and the feel of combat seemed to unwind the tension in the superbly trained Louis. He landed several left hooks and brought over a smashing right to the jaw. Schmeling was hurt. He retreated to the ropes, his right arm hooked over the top strand, his chin resting on it, three-quarters of his back exposed to his tormentor. Louis hit him with both hands, particularly the right, which smashed into Schmeling's body. Referee Donovan leaped in and started to count, though Schmeling was on his feet.

[96]

Now, staggering, Schmeling somehow moved toward the center of the ring. The noise of the crowd—one long, piercing shriek—overcame any sound in the ring. Louis was on Schmeling again, first with a left and then with an awesome right to the jaw. Schmeling went down, dazed and pained. He took a count of three. When he arose, Louis was still there, his nostrils flaring, his usually placid face now grim with determination. He smashed both hands to the German's head. Schmeling went down softly, his gloves just about touching the canvas, his knees bent. Somehow, he arose again. Again, Louis knocked him down. A towel—once recognized in boxing as a sign of surrender but no longer valid in New York State—was tossed into the ring by Machon. The referee, counting over Schmeling, somehow kicked the soggy towel backward with the heel of his right foot. It hit the ropes and hung on the middle strand, limp and unavailing. Donovan counted to five. Then, realizing Schmeling was through, he stopped the fight. Time consumed: two minutes and four seconds of the first round.

Louis allowed himself a smile as he went back to his corner. His coterie was in the ring, jumping all over him. He sat on his stool; and presently Schmeling, still dazed, came across the ring and put his arm around Louis and smiled. In Germany, Helmers's description of the end of the fight was never heard. When Schmeling had gone down for the first time, somebody pulled the master switch which controlled the Third Reich's radio network.

In his dressing room, Louis was surrounded by newspapermen. They wanted him to say that he hated Schmeling. He didn't. "I opened him up with those left jabs," he said. He would not claim that he had disproved Hitler's theory of a master race. His victory said it for him. He had many visitors. One of them was Frank Murphy, governor of Louis's home state of Michigan.

"Michigan is proud of you," the governor said.

"Thanks, Mr. Murphy," Louis said.

Then Louis went back to Harlem, riding in a limousine through streets filled with reveling supporters. The jubilation was nationwide.

Marva was at a friend's apartment on Saint Nicholas Avenue. He met her there, and they celebrated his victory. She had bet $15 that he would knock out Schmeling within four rounds. She collected.

The next day Louis went down to Mike Jacobs's office and talked to the reporters. Mike Jacobs told him his purse would come to $349,228. He was pleased, but mostly he was pleased because he had wiped out the memory of his knockout by Schmeling. He knew now that he was an authentic champion.

14

It was the last day of January 1969, and Freddie Wilson was worried. For the past two weeks, Louis had refused to leave his suite at the Park Sheraton Hotel. He had been visited there by Helen Dayton, and there had been a scene. In the course of an argument with her, he had ripped off her clothes. Detached from reality, he accused Miss Dayton of plotting his destruction and insisted she was conniving with the Mafia to have him killed while he slept. Wilson, Louis's faithful former sparring partner, finally decided to call Dr. Bennett in Detroit. He told him what had happened.

"Can't do a thing with him," Wilson said. "He's blown his top. You'd better come out."

"Be there in the morning," Dr. Bennett said.

"Guinyard comin' with you?"

"We'll be there."

Dr. Bennett had been Louis's physician for years, almost from the beginning of the fighter's career, and had been with him in one training camp after another. When Louis was visiting in Detroit, he frequently stayed at Dr. Bennett's spacious home on West Boston Boulevard. The physician had even worked in Louis's corner as a second. The thought, acutely painful, came to Dr. Bennett's mind: "Something's really wrong with Joe. He's always been humble and appreciative of other people, and now he is beginning to hate people, even those closest to him."

When Dr. Bennett and Guinyard arrived at the Park Sheraton the next morning, they found Louis in a state of terror. He said his body was wracked by pain.

"Let me examine you, Joe," Dr. Bennett suggested.

"Naw," Louis said. He was gruff.

"Have you been sleeping?"

"Ain't slept in two weeks," Louis said.

Then, extremely tense, he unburdened himself of a fantasy involving a Texan who had followed him into the suite to kill him. He found it difficult to breathe. Perspiration dampened his clothes and left beads on his forehead. He was hallucinating broadly, and repeatedly referred to Miss Dayton as the designer of the plot to murder him.

The fantasy assumed a related form. With his face contorted, he insisted that the walls of his bedroom were talking to him. "I gotta get a blackjack or a pistol," he said firmly, "I gotta protect myself." There was, for a moment, a mild digression. He lapsed into a vivid exposition of his sexual experiences. Then, over and over again, he repeated the tale of the Texan, of the sounds he heard coming from the walls, of his need to be protected against enemies obsessively delineated in his mind.

Finally, Dr. Bennett restored normal conversation. "All right, Joe," he said, "you're going to be all right. You've got some wrestling shows to referee. Why don't you get going on that?"

Louis explained that he had attempted at least half a dozen times to book plane reservations; but each time, at the last second, he had found it impossible to face the prospect of leaving the hotel.

"Ain't nothing wrong with you," Guinyard said. "And there's nobody following you. Nobody wants to kill you. Hell, everybody loves you, Joe."

Dr. Bennett was abruptly firm. "Look, Joe, you're coming out of this hotel."

"I ain't."

"Well, let me tell you this. Martha's on her way now. You can stay in and make a big scene, but she is on her way."

Louis was suddenly alert. He pulled on his clothes, picked up his overcoat and said, "God damn! Freddie, pack my stuff and meet me downstairs."

In the lobby, he ordered his car brought around to the hotel's Seventh Avenue entrance.

"Off he was in a second," Dr. Bennett remembers. "I used Martha's name to scare him. She wasn't coming in. He was afraid of her then. I don't think he is anymore."

15

Louis did not fear any man in the ring. But the Schmeling fight was his last in 1938. Emotionally exhausted, he needed relaxation from the rigors of training. He organized a softball team made up of youngsters from East Detroit. He paid all the bills, and it proved to be a costly venture. The team—the Brown Bombers—toured the country. Louis, on first base, was the major attraction; but when the season was over, he had lost $50,000 in the enterprise.

He had, by then, taken to riding show horses and, with Roxborough, purchased a 440-acre farm near Utica, Michigan. It was called Spring Hill Farm and became an attraction for blacks interested in horse shows. Louis even rode in one show at the farm. He went up on McDonald's Choice, owned by Marva, and won a ribbon by finishing in second place. "I always liked riding," he explained, "from when I was a kid in Alabama. It's fun." The way it turned out, Spring Hill Farm was one investment made by Louis that did not result in a financial loss. In 1946 the state of Michigan bought the property and turned it into a public park. Out of the proceeds Louis received the $8,500 he had invested in the land. "Beats losing," he said.

But in 1939 the money was going out as fast as it was coming in. Louis's wardrobe was extensive. He owned more than one hundred suits of clothing, some purchased at the extremely high cost of $175 each in New York and Chicago. He bought a Buick for his mother and a Studebaker for Vunies. Marva had a couple of cars and so did Joe. There were additional expenses. He was paying Vunies's way through Howard University and paying the mortgages on houses purchased for other members of his family. He opened a fried-chicken restaurant on Vernor Highway in East Detroit. It was run by a friend named Leonard Reed. The ill-fated venture cost Louis $25,000. Years later, when the government went to court to collect on Louis's income tax debt, one of his lawyers wrote a letter to the judge. It said, in part: "He has made large sums and has spent them. Where and how we do not completely know because Louis himself doesn't have this knowledge. At an early age he was schooled in profligacy instead of thrift. From the age of nineteen, he was surrounded by men of wealth who made money quickly and easily. During his championship period no brakes were applied to his spending."

There was a constant need for money; and Louis, in 1939, made four defenses of the championship. The first one brought Louis less gratification than any other bout in his career, and it resulted from speculations in the press concerning the champion's attitude toward fighting other Negroes.

For some time, John Henry Lewis, the world light-heavyweight champion, had been clamoring for a chance to fight Louis for the heavier title. When there was a delay in the match, sportswriters carelessly and callously suggested in print that Louis's handlers did not want him to go into the ring with another black man for fear of disturbing the Negro community's worship of Louis. The accusation was baseless. Louis was caught in a trap. He insisted that he did not want to fight John Henry only because they were friends. This profession of friendship was greeted with journalistic sneers. What Louis's handlers would not say was that the vision in John Henry Lewis's left eye was less than efficient and that Louis was afraid that his friend would be hurt in the ring. Still the newspapers persisted in their campaign in behalf of Lewis. So the match was made for Madison Square Garden in January 1939. Louis knocked his friend out in the first round. A right to the jaw flattened John Henry Lewis. Everybody in the Garden but the victim saw the punch coming. When the unhappy episode was over, Louis said, "That way he don't get hurt much. I don't like hitting no friend."

Three months later Louis knocked out Jack Roper in

one round in Los Angeles, after which Roper expressed himself so aptly his words are better remembered than the short-lived bout. "I zigged when I should of zagged," the victim said. Everybody laughed, but none more loudly than Louis. Tony Galento was Louis's next victim. "I'll knock da bum out," Galento promised, speaking through beer-stained lips. He was short and rotund and was called "Two-Ton Tony." Only friends and relatives accorded him a chance to take the title. The ticket sale was slow until Galento's manager, Joe Jacobs, leveled a fallacious charge against Louis.

Joe Jacobs was not related to Mike Jacobs, but he was the promoter's equal in terms of gall. He had been Schmeling's manager; and although he was a Jew, he had gone to Nazi Germany to work with Schmeling in a Hamburg ring. The fighter in the other corner was an American named Steve Hamas, who had, earlier, beaten Schmeling. When Schmeling knocked out Hamas in the ninth round in Hamburg, Joe Jacobs jumped into the ring and raised his arm in the Nazi salute even while puffing on a large cigar grimly clenched between his teeth.

Now, as Galento's manager, Joe Jacobs accused Louis of having used a "gimmick" on the night he knocked out Schmeling. The gimmick, Joe Jacobs charged falsely, was a metal bar which Louis had grasped in his right glove just before the opening bell. Outrage flared even in the insensitive world of boxing. Mike Jacobs was justifiably indignant. In concert with the New York State Athletic Commission, he demanded a retraction. It was made immediately. Nevertheless, the story got into print and spurred the sale of tickets for the fight.

Louis regarded Galento as a "funny little fat man," but in the ring at Yankee Stadium he learned otherwise. Galento, swinging from the floor, leaped at him with a left hook in the third round. It caught Louis on the right side of the jaw. He went down backward, landing awkwardly as a stunned crowd of 35,000 persons reacted almost silently. Then, hastily composed and determined, Louis arose. He hit Galento with smashing punches thrown in clusters. Each blow put a nick in Galento's pulpy face. Blood did not spurt. Rather, it trickled in the way blood does from a face nicked by a man foolhardy enough to shave himself carelessly with a straight razor. By the fourth round, the fight was over. Louis had earned $114,-332 for knocking out Galento.

Three more months passed, and Louis was in the ring again, this time in Detroit, where Louis caught up with Bob Pastor. In their first fight, before Louis was the champion, Pastor had run for ten rounds. The failure to knock out Pastor had caused Louis some embarrassment, and he had thought about it often, roaming in his imagination through another fight with Pastor in which he proved that speed could be offset by a solid punch on the jaw.

In the Detroit fight, Pastor altered his strategy. Instead of moving protectively, he carried the fight to Louis and was quickly knocked down. Weathering the storm, he began to move more alertly. Round after round went into the record book. At the end of the tenth round, Blackburn bawled out Louis. "You're hittin' him one punch at a time," the trainer scolded the champion. "Put 'em together. You're lazy, man." Louis went out in the eleventh round and flattened Pastor. He was paid $118,400 by promoter Jacobs. The "profligacy" in which he had been schooled took care of the money. He wasn't spending much time with Marva in Chicago. What he was spending was money. He bought one of his sweethearts a mink coat. Mike Jacobs got it for him wholesale. It cost $10,000. In the matter of excesses, as well as in the ring, Louis was a genuine champion.

16

Grim information came to Martha Louis. It produced in her a reaction of amazement and profound concern. Speaking of it later, Mrs. Louis said, "I was in New York, at the Park Sheraton, and I got this call from a girl, a prostitute. She said she wanted to see me, to talk to me. She came to see me and said she worked in a house run by a madame everybody called 'Momma.' She said Momma was a very nice woman and that she had discussed a certain situation with Momma before calling me. Momma told her to come and see me, as Joe's wife, to tell me about it. This girl told me that Joe was using cocaine occasionally. She said she knew all about Joe and Marie

Johnson and that it made her feel bad that an idol like Joe was being moved around by this Marie. She said Marie was very young and didn't realize how important Joe was. She said she hated to see Joe, with his name and reputation, become, using her language, 'fucked-up by some whore on narcotics.'

"She knew she could be frank with me because I've had a criminal law practice for years. These people will level with you generally because your reputation gets around. She said to me, 'I don't want you to hold anything against Joe because Joe is not responsible for what he's doing.' I didn't know what to do with the information. I was reluctant to confront Joe. I didn't go to him immediately with this girl's story. But one day I turned the conversation around to it. I said, 'Joe, did you have any experience with drugs of any kind?' He said, 'Oh, no. I wouldn't do anything like that.'

"When I really felt there was some truth in this girl's story was when Joe stayed out of the hotel a couple of nights and then came back with the tale that he had been in a place that was raided and had been put in jail. Then, one night, I got a call from a girl in Las Vegas. She said Joe was in a room with nothing but tramps and that they were having a coke party. When she told Joe she was going to call me, he laughed at her and chased her out of the room. When I saw Joe, I told him about this girl's call. He admitted everything except the narcotics aspect.

"Then I began noticing his actions, his mannerisms. Occasionally, his nose would be red, and he'd be sniffling. I'd say, 'Joe, what's the matter. Do you have a cold?' And he'd always say he had a cold. But that was it. I never saw him use cocaine. Once, when I was talking to him about it, I said, 'If you've got a problem, why don't you face up to it? I'll help you. I'm not only your wife, I'm your friend. I think I've proved that through the years.' He said, 'I know, I know you are, Martha.' "

17

When in 1940 Louis embarked on a busy fight schedule, Jack Miley, an imaginative sports columnist
for the *New York Post,* labeled it the "Bum-of-the-Month
Club." It was a misnomer, a pejorative composed out of
a need to be jocular. Actually, Louis simply went about
the task of proving conclusively that he was a fighting
champion. There was another urgent factor involved.
World War II had started in Europe, and there was a
widespread belief that the United States would become
involved eventually. Against that probability, Mike Jacobs
proposed a series of four fights that year. Obviously, profit
was his motive.

The first fight took place in Madison Square Garden, where Louis encountered a Chilean named Arturo Godoy. In retrospect Louis would recall it as a bout in which he was victimized by indifference. "In my first fight with Godoy," he remembered, "I really dogged it. I didn't feel peppy. Godoy had a funny crouch, and he was hard to hit; but that wasn't all that was wrong. I had no heart for fighting that night. That's why he stayed the fifteen rounds."

Immediately, there was a proposal for a return match. Instead, Louis took on a forlorn midwesterner named Johnny Paychek. In the hinterlands, Paychek had been knocking out many second-rate fighters, and his record was numerically impressive. In point of fact, he was hardly in Louis's class. Joe disposed of him in two rounds. Three months later, he was in the ring with Godoy again. It took him eight rounds to prove that he was Godoy's master. Louis smashed the South American's face; and when the referee, Billy Cavanaugh, stopped the fight, Godoy's torso was smeared with blood from cuts above both eyes.

Army camps throughout the country were filling with recruits. Louis himself had registered for the draft at Local Board 8 in Chicago. He went on a tour of eight camps and gave boxing exhibitions. Then, by way of finishing out the year, he knocked out Al McCoy in the Boston Garden on December 16. Six weeks later, on the last day of January 1941, he knocked out Red Burman in five rounds in Madison Square Garden. The "Bum-of-the-Month Club" was in full swing. In February, Louis knocked out Gus Dorazio in Philadelphia. He went to

[112]

Detroit in March and stopped a giant of a man named Abe Simon in thirteen rounds. Within three weeks, on April 8, he knocked out Tony Musto in St. Louis. The May party was in Washington, D.C., where he encountered Buddy Baer, Max's younger brother.

Buddy Baer was not his brother's equal in the ring. He was taller and heavier than Max, but he could not box as well and never achieved his brother's status. Yet, he did surprisingly well against Louis. Right in the first round, he hit Louis hard enough to send the heavyweight champion sprawling through the ropes. When Louis found his way back into the ring, Buddy Baer assaulted him with both fists; but Louis soon took control of the contest. By the sixth round, he was hitting his opponent at will. Buddy Baer went down three times in that round, the last knockdown coming just as the bell sounded. Buddy Baer's faction insisted the punch was illegal because it had been thrown after the bell and demanded that referee Donovan disqualify Louis. Donovan rejected their demand. Then, suddenly, there appeared in the ring a diminutive man wearing a porkpie straw hat. He climbed the steps in Buddy Baer's corner and, wedging his way between the ropes, scampered toward Louis's corner and disappeared down the stairs. It was Freddie Guinyard, Louis's friend. Guinyard, thinking the fight was over, had simply gone into the ring to congratulate the champion.

"He's with Louis," yelled Ray Arcel, Buddy Baer's trainer. "Why don't you disqualify Louis for that?"

Donovan ignored Arcel; but when Baer refused to answer the bell for the seventh round, he disqualified the challenger and awarded the bout to Louis.

Louis had worked hard. Within five months he had engaged in five fights. Training had drained him of energy. He needed a rest. But he was scheduled to fight Billy Conn at the Polo Grounds in New York City on July 18, and the prospect of a large purse lured him. He had not made too much money in 1941. The "Bum-of-the-Month Club" had produced total purses of just over $113,000. After taxes and the fifty-fifty split with Roxborough and Black, there was precious little left to keep Louis and his family living in the manner to which they had become accustomed. The fight promised a rich purse because Conn, the world light-heavyweight champion, was a magnetic figure in boxing.

Two years before, on the occasion of the literary baptism of the "Bum-of-the-Month Club," Miley had made this remarkable prophecy in prose: "Not so long ago a skinny, elbowy middleweight, William David Conn is growing like a weed. Now he's a light heavyweight, the champion of his class. When he cleans up those boys—and it won't be long—he will pick on Bob Pastor and any of the heavyweights who stand in his way. They won't hit him enough to hurt him . . . and by 1941 Louis will be even more jaded from fighting all the bums. And Conn will astound with his fearlessness, his speed. Heigh-ho, it is written in the cards, mates."

Miley's augury was exactly accurate. Conn's challenge of Louis had developed in accordance with Miley's prediction. And when it happened, it produced a spectacular bout in which Louis came close to losing the title he had safeguarded through a record number of seventeen defenses. Of his championship bouts, Louis had won fifteen by knockout. He was only twenty-seven years of age and never ill-used as a fighter. Except for the first misadventure against Schmeling, he had not taken a thorough beating. He was confident, though never contemptuous, and the aura of sweet victory enveloped him in the minds of all who believed him to be invincible.

The casting for Louis's bout with Conn was singularly attractive. Conn was a brash Irishman of twenty-three years, a loose-limbed boxer out of the East Liberty section of Pittsburgh. His belief in his ability as a fighter was total. In East Liberty he had learned to fight in streets teeming with the progeny of tough steelworkers. But he was not a brawler. His skill in the ring was consummate. He moved with an arrogant grace, bewildering his opponents by hitting them with an assortment of punches delivered from a multiplicity of angles.

Louis trained at Pompton Lakes. Newspapermen hung on his every word. When one of them suggested that Conn was too fast for him, Louis responded, "He can run, but he can't hide." The pithy rejoinder received widespread attention in the press. Blackburn was apprehensive. The trainer insisted that Louis should train for the Conn fight much as he had trained for all his other bouts, that there should be no attempt to match Conn's speed. Blackburn insisted that power would be decisive in the end. Fighter and trainer had a mild falling out. Instead of weighing over 200 pounds for the fight, Louis came in at 199½ pounds. He had, against Blackburn's wishes, "dried out" for two days—refrained from any liquids. He believed the lesser weight would enable him to move almost as swiftly as Conn, who actually weighed 168 pounds, although public announcement was made that it was 174 pounds.

The fight went on in ideal weather before 54,487 persons. Promoter Jacobs, frankly admitting in advance that he would not be disappointed if Conn won, supervised the counting of the receipts gleefully. There was $451,743 in the treasury. When Conn came into the ring, a great shout was heard in the old Polo Grounds. He appeared defiant, though boyish of mien. When Louis arrived in the ring, a thunderous roar of acclaim echoed in the ballpark. It was a sound he had often heard and had always accepted gracefully. No smile altered his countenance. But the bright lights of the ring caught his magnificent body in its muscular brilliance and abruptly made Conn appear puny by contrast.

And when they came together in the center of the ring after the opening bell, it appeared that Louis would make a short night's work of it. He stalked Conn, and the young challenger backed away nervously. Louis threw a long right. Conn, stumbling, slipped to the canvas. He hadn't been hit. He was jittery. By the second round, Conn had regained his composure. He began landing his left jabs and offsetting Louis's right counters with his own swift right fist. He had taken command. In the corner, after the fourth round, Blackburn berated Louis. "Take charge," the old trainer said. "Press him." So Louis went out for the fifth round and punished Conn with left hooks to the head and smashing rights to the body. The next two rounds were clearly the champion's. But there was a change in the wind. Suddenly, Conn was landing his jabs and moving away before Louis could respond. The champion appeared to weaken under the pace. The "drying out" process had deprived him of stamina. Going into the tenth round, it seemed Conn held full sway in the contest. And, in that round, he more than held his own, although Louis pressed him into corners and belabored his body.

Two-thirds of the fight had run its scheduled course, and Conn was still upright, indeed possibly in the lead on the scorecards of the two judges and referee Eddie Joseph. Sensing this, Conn went after Louis in the eleventh and twelfth rounds, raking the bigger man with left hooks. Once, disdaining discretion, he even led with his right and caught Louis full on the face. The crowd roared. Conn scored with a left and a right to the head. Louis was rocky. The bell rang.

Now, with the thirteenth round coming up, the crowd was in a frenzy. Conn was caught up in the sweep of emotions. He rushed out at the bell and attacked Louis. For two minutes, he engaged the champion in a slugging duel. Then, relaxing for a moment, he tried a hook to the champion's face, throwing it rather carelessly. Louis countered with a right over the left hook. It caught Conn full on the left temple and he wavered. Instinctively, he replied with a flurry of punches, and Louis, startled, lost a momentary advantage.

Less than a minute remained in the three-minute round. They moved to the center of the ring. Conn brashly started a left hook to Louis's head. It failed to reach its mark. In an instant, Louis retaliated with his right fist. It went over Conn's left arm and caught the challenger's jaw with full force. Conn was shaken, but still responsive. He pushed his right fist toward Louis. Instantly, Louis let his own right hand flash under the hot lights. Two more rights found Conn's head. And there was blood flowing from his nostrils and from a cut under his right eye. Stunned, he sought relief in a clinch. Louis pushed him off and hit him twice. Slowly, Conn went to the canvas, reaching for the ring floor with his left glove, straining for balance. The referee picked up the count. Conn, at the count of seven, came to his knees. He struggled to rise but was still down when the count reached ten. Only two seconds of the thirteenth round remained.

Conn's courage was indisputable. He had taken Louis a long way and was leading the champion on points on all three official scorecards. Indeed, if he had survived through the fifteen rounds and had won either the fourteenth round or the fifteenth round, he would have taken the title from Louis. His Irish spirit, journalists insisted, had cost him the heavyweight championship. Jacobs found cause to smile. A return bout between Louis and Conn promised riches even beyond *his* greedy aspirations.

Two days after the fight, Germany and Italy ordered all American consulates closed in their countries. New York City began training air raid wardens. And Louis had another fight scheduled. He fought Lou Nova on September 29 and knocked him out in six rounds. The occasion is memorable only because Louis, for the first time in the ring, altered his immobile expression. At one point, Nova's attempts to hit Louis with his right fist were so feeble, the champion stepped back and permitted himself the luxury of a laugh. The alteration in countenance did not imply derision. It was just great fun, that's all. Louis obviously was enjoying himself.

Little more than ten weeks later, the Japanese bombed Pearl Harbor. Even with the country at war, the controversy over Louis's knockout of Conn continued to rage among historians of sports. Had Conn been knocked out only because his Irish spirit had involved him in a needless exchange with Louis? Five years would pass before the issue would be settled.

18

Daylight had not yet brightened the sky over Detroit on March 20, 1969. At 2215 West Boston Boulevard there was an insistent knocking on the front door. Awakened from her sleep, the maid in Dr. Bennett's household was startled. Then, brushing sleep from her eyes, she answered the summoning sounds.

"Oh, it's you, Mr. Louis," she said, quickly conscious of something uncommon in his manner. His clothes were disheveled and his face distorted by fear. Apprehensive, she said, "I'll go wake Dr. Bennett."

Louis came into the house, dropped his luggage in the foyer and went to a window in the living room. He parted the curtains and peered into the street. That is where Dr. Bennett found him.

"What's the matter, champ?" Dr. Bennett asked.

"I ducked them," Louis said.

"What are you talking about?"

"Four men followed me from Chicago."

"Oh, Joe, there's nobody following you," Dr. Bennett insisted.

"They got on the same plane from Chicago and sat in the back. I got a cab, told the driver, 'Drive me to Dr. Bennett's house.' I said, 'Keep going, keep going, I'll pay you anything.' "

"All right, champ, you're safe here," Dr. Bennett said. "What happened in Chicago?"

"I was in Robert's Motel. The four men kept watching me. I went to their room. They weren't there. I tore up the room."

He slumped into a chair, and Dr. Bennett said, "Don't worry about that, champ. It'll be taken care of."

Louis was Dr. Bennett's house guest for five days. He talked frequently about people who were following him, who were determined to destroy him. His conversation followed the same pattern it had assumed when Dr. Bennett had gone to New York to see him a month before. But now the hallucinations and illusions Louis formed were deeper and broader. Then, when he seemed to be at his worst, the symptoms virtually disappeared. His conversation was logical. But at night the symptoms would return. Louis paced his bedroom floor incessantly. Twice in the course of his visit he awakened the household with his screams.

The first time, Dr. Bennett rushed to Louis's room. "What's wrong, champ?" he asked. To which Louis responded, "I thought those guys were in the room here." Dr. Bennett spoke to Louis in tranquilizing tones. The next time it happened Dr. Bennett and the others in the house simply ignored the screams. But the big question remained: What to do about Louis's illness? He sat down and wrote a letter to Martha Louis. When she received it in Los Angeles, she was struck by the last paragraph. "Joe is obsessed with many strange ideas and hallucinations," the physician wrote. "Immediate help should be instituted." Martha, sleepless in the dawn hours, wondered where to turn for help.

19

In the weeks after Pearl Harbor, while the nation was coming to the difficult realization that America was at war, Joe Louis was in training for a return bout with Buddy Baer. It was to take place in Madison Square Garden on January 9, 1942, and was remarkable because it was the first time that a world heavyweight champion would defend his title without any remuneration. All proceeds from the fight were to go to the Navy Relief Society. It was, on Louis's part, an especially significant gesture because blacks were treated even more unfairly in the navy than in the army. Only the most menial assignments were given them; and while Louis knew this, he was hopeful that his charitable gesture would ameliorate the circumstances in which his black brothers found themselves in the navy. By and large, Louis's contribution to the navy charity presumably did nothing immediately to alter bigotry in that branch of the service. But with the country at war it appeared to be the right thing to do. The onset of the war had brought a euphoria of unanimity to the land, and people willy-nilly came to believe that social injustice would suddenly disappear. So Louis went into the ring against Baer; and just before the start of the fight, Wendell Willkie climbed through the ropes.

Louis, who liked Willkie, greeted him with a smile. In the 1940 presidential election the champion had come out for Willkie against Roosevelt. He had even made some speeches in behalf of the Republican candidate. Now it was Willkie's turn. He went to the ring microphone and in the presence of 16,689 persons addressed Louis: "Thank you, Joe Louis, in the name of the United States Navy and the American people. Thank you for your magnificent contribution and the generosity in risking for nothing a title you have won through blood, sweat, and toil."

Jack Blackburn was in Louis's corner. The old trainer had been ailing and barely made it to Louis's training camp at Greenwood Lake, New York. Before the fight he told Joe, "My heart's bad. I don't think I can make those stairs tonight." Louis responded, "You won't have to climb those steps but once, Chappie."

And that's the way it was. Louis flattened Baer in the first round. He was in no mood for a long fight—marital problems were on his mind. Some months earlier Marva had filed a divorce suit in Chicago. When the news broke, Louis was on a golf course in Detroit.

"Joe, your wife just sued you for divorce," a reporter told him.

"No kiddin'," Louis said.

"She says you hit her twice."

He was incredulous. "Why she say that?"

In truth, Marva was unhappy because Louis was neglecting her. He had, for example, promised to meet her in Chicago after the fight with Conn. He had instead gone to Detroit. So she filed for divorce, and it was Louis's first inclination not to contest the suit. But when she demanded half of his assets and half of all his future earnings as alimony, he went to court in Chicago. There was an absence of acrimony on both sides. And when the couple appeared before a master in chancery to determine just how much alimony Marva was entitled to, the attorneys for both sides announced that neither Joe nor Marva wanted to continue the action. A recess was called and husband and wife went into an adjoining room for a conference. A short time later, they emerged. Louis was carrying Marva in his arms. While flashlights lit the scene, a reporter asked Louis what had happened. "It's just like getting married again," the champion said buoyantly. "We're going home."

And so the passage at law ended. But its cause—Louis's neglect of Marva—persisted. It bothered her. It bothered him. Louis had gone into training for the Nova fight almost immediately after the bout with Conn. Then the fight with Baer was imminent, and he had to leave Marva alone. And now an even more insistent assignment was at hand. It would occupy Louis for the next four years.

The day after the fight with Baer, Louis received a notice from his Chicago draft board. It ordered him to appear there for induction into the army. Immediately, Louis waived all rights to delay his induction. He made only one request. Would the Chicago board allow him to take his physical examination in New York? The concession was made immediately. A few days later, Louis took a ferry to Governors Island in New York Harbor and underwent examination. The conclusion was foregone. He was fit for military duty. The place of his examination was bedlam. Reporters and photographers competed for position near the champion. They pushed aside military brass to get their stories and their pictures. The next day, January 12, 1942, the scene was repeated at Camp Upton, Yaphank, Long Island. Busloads of newsmen trailed Louis to the camp. It had snowed, and the military post was a quagmire. The champion took it all in stride, quietly posing for his first pictures in uniform. Indeed, he had asked that his induction be accomplished quietly, without the presence of the press. But army morale officers insisted he was too important a person to slip into khaki quietly. The next day, *The New York Times* took editorial note of his induction at a time when he could be making hundreds of thousands of dollars in the ring. "He is cheerfully giving up that much, minus his army pay, to serve his country," the editorial suggested. "If any of us resent our present and prospective burden of war taxes we might think of Joe Louis's contribution. His championship now is more than of the prize ring: he is a champion citizen."

A month before Louis's induction into the army, the Boxing Writers Association of New York had accorded Louis its highest honor: the Edward J. Neil Memorial Plaque, named in memory of a colleague who had been killed while covering the Civil War in Spain. Presentation of the award was made at a dinner at Ruppert's Brewery, a formidable Manhattan edifice since destroyed by the wrecker's hammer. But then, on January 21, 1942, it was the site of an impressive ingathering of boxing's supporters. The dais groaned under the presence of J. Edgar Hoover, director of the Federal Bureau of Investigation; James J. (Jimmy) Walker, former mayor of New York City; and Jack Dempsey, Gene Tunney, and Jimmy Braddock, all former heavyweight champions.

Walker, a sentimentalist, was invited to present the major award of the evening to Louis. He sensed the mood of the party. Alcohol in abundance had been consumed, and good cheer was pervasive. Always long-winded, he lost no time in delivering a lengthy speech. Then, by way of peroration, he said: "Joe, all the Negroes in the world are proud of you because you have given them reason to be proud. You never forgot your own people. You are an American gentleman. When you fought Buddy Baer and gave your purse to the Navy Relief Society, you took your title and your future and bet it all on patriotism and love of country." Then, indulging in a pause to drain the last drop of sentiment from his words, he added, "Joe Louis, that night you laid a rose on the grave of Abraham Lincoln."

Louis came toward the microphone. This man, who as a boy had chopped cotton in an Alabama patch, was in competition with a master orator. He chose the right verbal path, the only one open to him—simplicity of statement.

"You don't know how you make me feel," he said. "The way I feel is good. I never thought I'd feel so good as when I won the heavyweight championship of the world, but tonight tops them all. I feel better than I ever felt in my life. Thanks for what you did for me. I want to thank Mike Jacobs for what he did for me. I want to thank the boxing commission for what it did for me. I hope I never did anything in the ring I'll be sorry for in the years to come. I'm a happy man tonight."

The old room in which the dinner was held resounded with applause. The sound bounced off the oak-hewn ceiling. And the most responsive persons in the room were in Louis's faction, comprising his managers and sparring partners and other employees. Only old Jack Blackburn was not there. His doctors had refused him permission to come on from Chicago. A faltering heart had tied him to his bed. And he would not be there when his pupil would make his last defense of the heavyweight championship while America was at war.

Louis went back to Camp Upton after the dinner and applied himself to the task of soldiering. He asked that he be treated no differently than the other recruits. He learned how to dig foxholes, and he learned the manual of arms. He fired on the pistol and rifle ranges and proved a good shot. No quarter asked, no quarter granted; he was a soldier in the United States Army. But he was still the heavyweight champion; and the army, aware of his bout with Buddy Baer for the benefit of the Navy Relief Society, now suggested that he box in behalf of the Army Relief Society. Not lost on army brass was the fact that Louis's entire purse of $65,200 had gone to the other service's charity.

It was arranged for Louis to fight Abe Simon in Madison Square Garden on March 27, 1942. This one would enrich the Army Relief Society. Louis was transferred to Fort Dix in New Jersey, where a new $85,000 gymnasium had been built. Louis would have preferred to train at Pompton Lakes, but the costs were prohibitive. Expenses for a training siege there always cost about $50,-000, involving expenses for sparring partners, rent, transportation, and food. At Fort Dix the cost came to $18,000. For Louis the training grind was different. Blackburn was absent, though he had tried to get there from Hot Springs, Arkansas, where he had gone to recuperate. He felt better than he had in Chicago, but he was still not strong enough to make the trip. So Mannie Seamon, who had been Blackburn's assistant, took over the task of training Louis. Seamon had been with Louis a long time, and the fighter liked him. He had grown up in boxing in the days of Benny Leonard, the great old champion he had trained, and knew his way around the game. He worked hard to get Louis in shape for the fight with Simon.

This was not easy. Working at an army post posed problems. Louis, for one, was still required to do two hours of military training under the guidance of Corporal Robert A. Shaw, a member of Company L, Louis's outfit at Camp Upton. This obtruded on his training schedule, which, as always, he began each morning by running six or eight miles. But he felt good. More than 3,000 soldiers

[129]

would attend his sparring sessions each day, and the thought that he was entertaining them pleased him. He worked hard and got down to 207½ pounds.

The morning of the fight he telephoned Blackburn, who was now in Provident Hospital in Chicago.

"I'm in shape," he told Blackburn.

"You got your weight down?"

"I'm okay," Joe said.

"Just keep after him. You'll knock him out," Blackburn said.

Louis bought several thousand tickets for the fight and distributed them to soldiers at Camp Upton. Going into the ring that night, he looked around the arena and spotted his friends in khaki. He was warmed by their presence. Then he looked over at Simon in the other corner. The enemy weighed 255½ pounds. Louis thought, "I got to get him out of there fast." It took him a little longer than he had expected it to take. Simon, knocked down in the second and fifth rounds, was finished off early in the sixth round. Louis's purse was $45,882. It went to the Army Relief Society.

On the radio after the fight Louis spoke directly to Blackburn. "Keep punchin', Chappie," he said. A month later, Blackburn was dead. Louis was given permission to leave Camp Upton to attend the funeral in Chicago. "I loved that Chappie," he told newspapermen.

There came a night when he went to Madison Square Garden to attend a Navy Relief Society benefit show. He was accompanied by Billy Rowe, an able correspondent for the *Pittsburgh Courier*, a Negro newspaper. They had become close friends when Louis had first come to New

York to fight Primo Carnera; and later they would become partners in a public relations company in New York. But then, on that night in 1942, they were just good friends.

"What'll you say if they call on you to speak?" Rowe asked Louis.

"I'll think of something," Louis said. "Always do."

Now Louis was on stage, straining to express himself. He opened his short speech slowly and gained confidence as he went along. Then, for an ending, he expressed the confidence of a nation at war. "We can't lose because we're on God's side," he said. The audience rose and cheered.

"How'd I do?" he chided Rowe when he returned to his seat.

"You're a dummy," Rowe said. "You should know it doesn't go that way. You got the saying all wrong. The saying is, 'We're going to win because God is on our side.' "

"Oh no," Louis said. "I made a mistake."

"You sure did," Rowe said. "I winced when you said it."

The next day the newspapers ran laudatory stories about Louis's speech. His inverted allusion to God as America's ally was praised everywhere.

"Who's the dummy now?" he asked Rowe.

20

"Immediate help should be instituted," Dr. Bennett's recommendation, repeated itself again and again in Martha's mind. Whenever she attempted to involve Louis in a conversation regarding his illness and the need for treatment, he compulsively restated all his fears, including the hallucinatory notion that Martha somehow was involved in the plot to poison him. So she refrained from outward manifestations of concern, though the problem was before her constantly; and whenever Louis decided to travel, she went with him. Late June 1969 found them in New York in pursuit of a business deal. A wealthy jewelry manufacturer named Abe Margolies had proposed, in

Louis's behalf, the formation of the Joe Louis Food Franchise Corporation. They were good friends, and Margolies had instituted the business deal to give Louis a constant source of income.

On June 26, Margolies summoned representatives of the news media to Les Champs, a restaurant off Madison Avenue. It was only reasonable that disclosure of Louis's venture into the food franchise business should be made in that richly decorated place. It was owned by Margolies, the prime mover in the new enterprise. Wall Street underwriters were prepared to float a stock issue for the new corporation, and franchises in a national chain of restaurants were to be sold to individual investors, each thereby privileged to use Joe Louis's magnetic name to lure customers.

Joe and Martha liked the deal. The underwriters already had written out a check for $10,000 and had handed it to Martha. Besides, Louis had insisted that Billy Conn, his old ring rival, be involved in the undertaking. So Conn had picked up a check for $1,500 from the underwriters; and when announcement of the new corporation was made, Conn was at Louis's side.

The next morning, Louis went to a studio in Times Square to appear on the "Joe Franklin Show," a local television talk program. Martha and Margolies were with him, along with Leo Charney, Margolies's attorney, and Kiah Sayles, another of Louis's good friends. Video-taping of the show under hot lights consumed more than an hour, and when it was over, they all proceeded downtown to keep an appointment with Percy Sutton, the borough president of Manhattan.

They rode in Charney's car. When they were within one block of the borough president's office off City Hall Park, Louis complained that he was ill. Perspiration ran down his face. He was bent over, mumbling about pains in his stomach. In a flash Margolies opened the door on his side of the car, and Louis followed him out. In his rush he almost tripped over Margolies.

"I think I'm dying," Louis gasped.

"You'll be all right, we'll get help," Margolies said.

Louis was leaning on a litter can for support. Sayles, leaving the car, herded Louis and Margolies back into the vehicle. "There's a hospital a couple of blocks away. Let's get there fast," Charney said.

He drove away quickly, ignoring stop signs and red lights. Within minutes the car was in front of the Beekman Downtown Hospital. Margolies leaped out of the car and rushed into the hospital.

"I got Joe Louis outside," he yelled. "He's very sick. It's an emergency."

Almost immediately, attendants pushing a stretcher on wheels were at Louis's side. They lifted him onto the vehicle and rolled him into the hospital. He was placed under intensive care, and a stomach pump was applied. In a flash newsmen were in the hospital clamoring for information. A nurse of large proportions kept them at bay. All she would tell them was that Louis's condition was "satisfactory." Martha went to a telephone and called Dr. Bennett in Detroit. He arrived the next morning armed with Louis's electrocardiogram. A new electrocardiogram was taken. Comparative studies did not disclose evidence of a heart attack.

"I ate two cantaloupes and drank a lot of milk for breakfast," Louis said. "I think that made me sick."

Several days later, he was back in Las Vegas. "What happened," he told newspapermen, "was all the running around in that humidity in New York made me sick."

He had offered two explanations of his collapse, neither accurate, and another year would pass before he would look back on the event and describe it accurately. But then, in June 1969, he was not yet ready to talk.

Not long after his collapse, the deal for formation of the Joe Louis Food Franchise Corporation also collapsed. "Wall Street was bad, and the public just wasn't going for franchise deals," Margolies explained. "I didn't want Joe's name associated with a flop."

21

L ouis was in the army five months when he was sent to
Fort Riley, Kansas. It was June 1942, and in the
interval between going into the army and his transfer to
Fort Riley, he had asked for cavalry duty. His love of
horses dictated the choice. Fort Riley was a cavalry post.
While taking basic training there, he ran into Jackie Robinson. Five years would pass before Robinson would become the first black player in major league baseball; but
then, in the army, he was just another black soldier endur-
ing prejudices that did not stop at the main gate to the fort.

Along with nineteen other blacks, Robinson had put
in an application for Officers Candidate School. For rea-

sons so obvious as to need no underlining here, the applications were stalled. Robinson told Louis about it. He explained that each of the blacks applying for training as officers had a college background. At the University of California at Los Angeles, Robinson had been a foremost varsity football player. But at Fort Riley he was just another black, subject to the bigotry of white officers.

Louis, incensed, rushed to a telephone. The person he put in a call to was Truman K. Gibson, a Chicago lawyer. He had known Gibson in Chicago and was aware that the lawyer was a special adviser on Negro affairs to the Secretary of War. Hearing Louis's story, Gibson immediately made the matter known to the War Department. But Louis did not stop there. He asked for permission to talk with Brigadier General Donald A. Robinson, commanding officer of the Cavalry Training Center at Fort Riley. Presently, in the general's presence, he expanded on the theme of racial prejudice in the army.

He told General Robinson he would not speak or box in any army camp in which black soldiers were victimized by Jim Crow regulations. And he urged the general to take action in behalf of black candidates for training as officers.

Jackie Robinson remembers the result of Louis's appeal to General Robinson. "Within a week—I say within a week, it could have been longer—we were in Officers Candidate School. All of the black candidates passed and became officers. It was my first experience with Louis. Later, when I went up to the majors with the Brooklyn Dodgers, people asked me if I would have made it if there hadn't been a Joe Louis before me. I think so, eventually. If I hadn't made it, some other black player would have.

[137]

But Joe, by his conduct, cleared the way. And it's a funny thing. Joe himself has never really realized the impact he had on the black community and the fight against prejudice."

Louis moved around a great deal in the army. He took a boxing troupe that included Sugar Ray Robinson, the splendid boxer, to Camp Sibert in Alabama. One afternoon, they went down to the bus station to telephone for a taxicab to take them to town. While waiting for the taxi, Louis sat on a bench in the station with Robinson. A military policeman ordered them to move to another bench in the rear. "That's for people like you," the MP insisted. Louis would not change his seat. Neither would Robinson. A provost marshal was summoned. In the commotion, Robinson wrapped his strong arms around one of the military policemen. He was screaming. Louis and Robinson were hustled off to the stockade. An officer bawled out Louis. "When an MP tells you to do something, you do it," he said. Louis responded coldly, "Sir, I'm a soldier like any other American soldier. I don't want to be pushed to the back because I'm Negro."

News of the incident got into the papers. In Washington the Inspector General's Office started an investigation. Soon thereafter, Jim Crow buses were outlawed in the army. But Louis found prejudice in other forms. He was made a sergeant and went overseas in 1943. The next year, while touring England with a troupe of boxers, he went to a civilian cinema. He was refused admission by the cashier. The theater's manager was summoned. Recognizing Louis, he explained that an American officer commanding the area had issued the order barring blacks from theaters frequented by white soldiers. An attempt was made to hush up the incident; but when word of it reached Lieutenant General John C. H. Lee, General Eisenhower's deputy, the Jim Crow order was rescinded. The officer who had instituted the practice was sent back to the United States.

Louis's boxing troupe entertained troops in Scotland, North Africa, Italy, and Alaska. In London he survived twelve successive nights of bombing by Hitler's V-1 rockets. In Italy he visited the front lines and was granted permission to pull the lanyard of a large artillery piece. The next day the gun blew up, killing several soldiers standing nearby. Once, flying over England with Billy Conn, the plane's landing gear stuck. For half an hour the craft circled over Liverpool. Apprehensively, Louis eyed Conn. Neither spoke. Finally, the captain piloting the plane indicated the landing gear had come unstuck. Conn said, "You were always a lucky guy, Joe. I want to stick close to you."

Even as a soldier, Louis did not alter his life-style. He borrowed money freely from Mike Jacobs, and was himself a soft touch for any soldier with a sob story. He had no more regard for the condition of his finances than he had when he was a civilian earning large sums of money in the ring.

At one juncture, Jacobs convinced the War Department that a return bout between Louis and Conn for the benefit of service charities would help sustain morale in a country fighting a major war. A committee of sportswriters was named by the War Department to supervise promotion of the bout by Jacobs. Then a storm broke. It was discovered that one of the conditions of the fight called for Jacobs to deduct Louis's debts to him from the proceeds. The secretary of war called off the bout.

While Joe was in the army, in March 1945, Marva Louis obtained an uncontested divorce. The grounds were desertion. As part of the alimony arrangement, Louis agreed to pay Marva one-quarter of all his future earnings in the ring. He had already made up his mind that Julian Black, Roxborough's managerial partner, would no longer share in his earnings as a fighter. This arrangement, almost casually agreed upon, would become a major factor in the income tax difficulties in which he would find himself later.

Louis was thirty-one years of age when he was discharged from the army in 1945. He had been out of the ring almost four years, years that would have been financially productive. Skills sharpened only by activity were dulled. And he was heavily in debt. No complaint parted his lips. He looked ahead to the second chapter in his history as a fighter. The army had brought about an alteration in his personality. Before he pulled on khaki, he had depended largely on his managers to make decisions for him. Now, apparently matured by his experiences as a soldier, he began thinking for himself. This did not mean that he would always arrive at the correct decision. But he was at last his own man.

22

The days after Louis's collapse in New York passed harmlessly. He went to Dayton, Ohio, and earned a fee as a commentator on a televised golf show. Then, returning to Las Vegas with Martha, he was once again severely delusional. He insisted that the Mafia was trying to poison him and refused to eat alone. When friends would sit at a dining table, he would wait until they had finished eating and then reach for the leftovers.

Abe Margolies's brother, Robby, visited Louis at Caesars Palace. "I remember it well," Robby Margolies said subsequently. "I was eating in the coffee shop, and Joe was with me. I ordered a steak, some cheesecake, and then some bananas and sour cream. Joe watched me eat. I didn't finish everything on the plates, but when I pushed the plates away, Joe began picking at what was left. When he came to the bananas and sour cream, he said, 'Who eats that?' I said, 'Jews.' He said, 'It's good enough to be soul food!' "

Martha found no humor in her husband's delusional concerns. One night she was awakened by sounds coming from the terrace outside their room at Caesars Palace. She went out into the cool air and detected Louis's huge frame outlined against the decorative cement scrollwork lining the terrace. Her husband was standing on a stool and pasting masking tape over the open portions of the scroll-work.

"What are you doing, Joe?" she asked.

"They're shooting air in through here," Louis said calmly. "I'm stopping up those cracks where those ass-holes are putting that poison stuff in on me."

Louis had been booked to referee a series of wrestling bouts throughout the South. Martha decided it might help him if he were to fulfill his obligation. The tour took them to many cities, starting with Dallas and winding up in Nashville, Tennessee. Whenever they stayed in a hotel with air conditioning, Louis would attempt to paste newspapers over the vents in his room. And when they would check out, he would go to the door of the room adjoining theirs and bang on it. "I'm leaving now," he would scream. "You satisfied?" The banging would get louder and louder, and Martha would cajole her husband into leaving the hotel.

While they were on the tour, on August 31, 1969, Rocky Marciano was killed in the crash of a private plane in Newtown, Iowa. The former heavyweight champion's body was shipped to Fort Lauderdale, Florida, for burial. Louis had always respected the heavily muscled boxer and, hearing of his death, insisted that he wanted to attend Marciano's funeral. So the Louises flew to Miami and stayed at the International Hotel at the airport. One afternoon, they had lunch in their room. For dessert Martha ordered cheesecake for two.

Louis ate a piece of his portion and then asked a busboy to wrap the remainder in paper.

"What are you going to do, Joe? Save that for dessert later?" Martha asked.

"Yes, yes, Martha." Then, placing the cake on the dresser, he added, "I'm going to the police with it."

"Going to the police? Why?"

"Those folks put some stuff in this cake."

"What kind of stuff?"

"Poison stuff," Louis insisted.

"Don't be silly. I ate it, too," she said firmly.

Louis reflected on this. "All right," he said. He did not carry out his threat to go to the police.

When the tour ended in Nashville, Martha asked Louis, "We going back to Los Angeles?"

"All right with me," he said. Later, he changed his mind. "I want to go to Las Vegas," he said with some self-assurance. But before long there was an alteration in his destination. "Let's go to Detroit," Louis said. "These people here have shot enough gas in on me to kill me. I'm sick. I want to go to Detroit to find out what's wrong with me."

She took this as a good sign. They headed for Detroit.

23

When Louis signed for his second fight with Conn, Marshall Miles was actively handling all managerial duties for the world heavyweight champion. Roxborough was still financially interested in Louis, but he had withdrawn from direct participation in the fighter's business affairs. During his time in the army, Louis had borrowed freely from Roxborough; and, apart from a sentimental attachment to his old friend, he felt obliged to continue their commercial association. As for Black, Louis had no compunction. No managerial contract was in existence, so he simply sacked Black and turned to Miles for advice.

Miles was Roxborough's friend. Years before, while on a trip to Detroit from his home in Buffalo, he had encountered the young fighter in Roxborough's office. "Come on, I want you to meet the next heavyweight champion of the world," Roxborough had said, and Miles had shaken the shy young man's hand. He thought, at that moment, "My gosh, they're certainly jumping the gun." That afternoon he went with Louis to see the Detroit Tigers play the St. Louis Cardinals in the opening game of the 1934 World Series. But in 1946, Miles suddenly found himself in the role of Louis's manager. Louis had simply come to see him while Miles was visiting his brother in Los Angeles and had suggested that Miles manage him. An agreement was reached, and by the time Louis climbed into the ring to fight Conn again at Yankee Stadium on June 19, 1946, Miles was firmly bound up in Louis's affairs.

Mike Jacobs was in a jubilant mood. For more than four years he had envisioned the financial killing he would perpetrate in connection with the second meeting of Louis and Conn. A war had obtrusively caused a delay; but now, with America once more devoted to peace, he savored thoughts of huge profits. He was the premier promoter of boxing in the world, and the Louis–Conn return, he believed, would establish his overlordship forever. So he set the price of ringside tickets at $100 each and predicted gross receipts of $3 million for Louis's twenty-second defense of the heavyweight title. All the while, he was not unmindful of another financial fact: Louis owed him $170,000. The fight would enable him to collect all or a major part of the debt.

Louis was thirty-two years old. He weighed 207 pounds to Conn's 187 pounds. And when they climbed into the ring for this second coming of Armageddon, only 45,266 persons were in Yankee Stadium, some 9,000 fewer than the crowd for their first meeting. Jacobs had simply overreached himself. The $100 ticket price was too rich even for the blood of postwar America.

Right from the opening bell, the fight was an anticlimax. So many had waited so long to see it, it simply could not live up to the sense of anticipation it had spread throughout the country. Conn was a hollow shell, though he was only twenty-seven years of age. The war had been a thief of his skills. Besides, in training he had worked so diligently to retrieve a measure of his old fire, he had developed painful blisters on his soles. He could hardly move. The first six rounds were a charade. Louis and Conn stared at each other, and the crowd booed. There was some milling in the seventh round, and the eighth round brought welcome surcease from boredom. Louis scored with a hard right to Conn's face. When he withdrew his glove, blood appeared from a cut under Conn's left eye. A right to the jaw whistled in the night air. It caught Conn on the jaw, and his knees buckled. In Louis's corner Mannie Seamon, his trainer, screamed, "Go get him, Joe!" The champion threw a left hook and a right cross. Both connected. Conn went down. The fight was over after two minutes and nineteen seconds of the eighth round.

When Jacobs counted the gross receipts, they came to $1,925,564, a most respectable number. But he had forecast receipts of $3 million; and the newspapers, having taken the promoter at his optimistic word, ridiculed the fight as a fistic and financial flop. For Louis it was a disaster that compounded his income tax difficulties.

His purse came to $591,116. Added to this was $5,818 from other sources of revenue, making a total of $596,935. Immediately, $115,992 was paid in federal income taxes. Another $28,692 went for New York State income taxes. His managers received $140,492. And the heaviest blow was the $204,000 in debt payments to Jacobs and Roxborough. In addition, in accordance with their alimony agreement, Marva Louis received $66,000, though she would remarry Joe a month later. The total came to $655,176. Louis was in hock. Four years later, the federal government would impose a further levy of $246,055 in taxes on the purse from the fight with Conn; but at the time, in 1946, Louis already had enough trouble to turn a more sensitive man's hair gray during a long day's night.

"When it was over," Miles remembers, "we still needed some more tax money. Joe had only a few dollars, not much; so I put $20,000 into the National City Bank in Times Square in his name. One day, I'm up in the Theresa Hotel, and the manager of the bank calls me. He says, 'Mr. Miles, Joe Louis was in here this morning and withdrew $10,000 and opened an account with it in a woman's name.' I couldn't believe it. I rushed down to the bank."

Once at the bank, Miles heard the rest of the story. Louis had, in fact, opened the account in a woman's name. Moreover, he had withdrawn $1,000 for himself. "Within a week," Miles insists, "the other $9,000 was gone. That's how he was, giving away a thousand here, a thousand there."

There was a need to get Louis some money quickly. But even more pressing was the federal government's insistent demand for more income tax payments. Miles sat down with Louis and explained the situation. It was decided that the champion would have one more fight in 1946, but that nobody would share in his purse except Mannie Seamon, his trainer, and other hired hands.

"Whatever you get, Joe, we'll leave with Mike Jacobs," Miles suggested. "Then, early next year, we'll use it to pay some more of your income taxes. In that way, we may be able to square the whole tax thing."

"It's all right with me," Louis said.

A young heavyweight named Tami Mauriello was chosen as Louis's opponent, and the fight was set for Yankee Stadium on September 18, 1946. It would be the Brown Bomber's twenty-third defense of the title. He had been the heavyweight champion for nine years, the longest reign in the history of the division; and he had defended the title more times than any of his predecessors. Against such a background, nobody would suggest that he had chosen to fight Mauriello because the young man was only a moderate fighter. The way it turned out, it was almost a disaster.

Mauriello walked out at the opening bell and proceeded to take liberties with the champion. Abruptly, he threw a sharp left hook that landed on Louis's jaw. Stunned, the champion was knocked against the ropes. Donovan, refereeing a title bout involving Louis for the twelfth time, stepped into Mauriello's path. By the time the referee and challenger were disentangled, Louis had recovered. He charged at Mauriello with both hands flying. Within two minutes and nine seconds of the first round, the fight was over. Louis had scored another knockout. The fight had drawn 38,494 persons. Gross receipts were $335,063. Of this sum, Louis was paid $103,-611. When matters were settled, Miles deposited almost $100,000 with Mike Jacobs. "We'll come and get it in January of next year," he told the promoter. "Just make sure it's all there."

In December 1946, Jacobs suffered a cerebral stroke. While he was convalescing, the affairs of the 20th Century Sporting Club were in the hands of Sol Strauss, his lawyer. One morning in January 1947, Miles arrived at the offices of the boxing corporation in Madison Square Garden. He greeted Rose Cohen, Jacobs's secretary, and told her he had come to get the money due Louis from the purse for the Mauriello fight. She appeared surprised.

"You'll have to wait until Mr. Strauss comes in," the secretary said. Miles detected a note of uncertainty in her voice.

A while later, Strauss arrived. Miles entered his office and told him the nature of his mission. "Just a minute," Strauss said. "Let me get Rose." He picked up a phone and summoned her. "Tell Marshall what happened," Strauss said, whereupon the secretary broke the sad news: Louis had withdrawn all but $500 of the purse for the bout with Mauriello. Canceled checks and Western Union money-order receipts, all made out in Louis's name, were shown to Miles. He left the office in a daze.

When he caught up with Louis, he demanded an

explanation. "Where did the money go?" he asked.

"Into the Rhum Boogie," Louis replied.

"Oh, no," the manager said.

The Rhum Boogie Café was a nightclub on Garfield Boulevard in Chicago. Louis had bought the place and had put his friend Leonard Reed, a black comedian, in charge. Some $40,000 had gone down the drain. There had been other extravagances; losses in bets in support of Louis's golfing skills had accounted for some of the money. And the cost of gifts for the ladies came high.

"Why did you leave $500 when you took all that other money?" Miles asked Louis.

No answer was heard. All Miles remembers was Louis's loud laughter. He did not view his profligacy as a tragedy. He never would.

24

September 17, 1969, Detroit, Michigan. Louis was in Kirwood Hospital at Forty-fifth and Madison. He and Martha had flown to Detroit together, but she had continued on to Los Angeles after Dr. Bennett had checked her husband into the hospital. When Martha returned to the hospital on Friday, September 19, Louis was morose. He was dressed and ready to check out. "I wouldn't put a dog in this place," he said. "I want to get out." Martha asked him, "Why do you want to leave?" He spoke quickly. "Everybody after me. That goes for Bennett too. Let's get out of here." They checked into the St. Regis Hotel.

They were scheduled the next morning to go to Oklahoma City, where Louis was to appear on a television show to promote a wrestling card in that area.

"I'm not going," he said. "I'm too sick. Those people are coming through the wall at me with dynamite."

Their suite was next to an elevator shaft. All night long he had listened to the squeal of the ascending and descending car. He found the sound foreboding.

Martha said, "I'll tell you what, Joe. Let's put on the television set, and then you won't hear the noise." When she did this, Louis complained that lightning was coming into the room through the television set.

The next day he was calm. It was Sunday, and he spent it at the home of his sister Vunies. She had always been his favorite. Formerly a teacher, she now counseled students in a Detroit high school. And she had four children of her own. In the pleasant domestic atmosphere of her home, Louis found some peace.

"Joe's a very sick man," Martha had told Vunies. "If he starts talking funny, pay no attention to him."

Nothing untoward happened, but late in the afternoon Martha received a telephone call from her husband. He was concerned about a report on the radio of a fire in the barn area of the Detroit Race Course. Some horses had perished in the blaze, and Louis knew that a friend, C. W. Smith, a Detroit industrialist and sportsman, stabled some of his thoroughbreds at the racetrack.

"Call him and see if his horses are all right," Louis told Martha. He was pleasant and contained. Later that evening, he returned to the St. Regis.

"None of Smitty's horses were in the fire," she told Louis. "Did you have a nice day?"

"Yeah," Louis said. A moment later he was distraught. "If those people start bothering me tonight," he threatened, "I'm leaving this place and going down to Sonny Wilson's hotel."

"That's all right with me," Martha said. "If you feel better at the Mark Twain, just go down there for the night. Whenever you get back, I'll be here."

By bedtime, Louis had changed his mind. But he would not sleep in the bedroom. "The place is full of gas they're shooting in on me," he said. He slept on a couch in the living room of their suite.

When he awakened the next morning, he told Martha he was in no shape to keep a date to referee a wrestling match that night in a town near Tulsa, Oklahoma.

"Those people shot enough gas in here on me to give me a heart attack. Take me to Ford's hospital."

Martha accompanied her husband to Henry Ford Hospital. In the admissions office Louis turned to Martha abruptly and said, "I know why they're asking me so many questions. They're stalling for the Mafia to get me."

"Oh, Joe," she responded. "These are just routine questions. They always ask these questions when you're admitted to a hospital."

"Go try and find Henry Ford and tell him what's happening," Louis said. Henry Ford II was a friend.

Martha went to a telephone and tried to call Ford. He was out of town. She went back to the admissions office and beckoned to the hospital worker who was filling out Louis's history. Off to a side, she whispered to him, "Don't ask Joe any more questions. Just get him a bed. He's a very sick man."

Martha suddenly remembered that one of C. W.

Smith's friends was a staff physician at the hospital. She went off to look for him, only to learn that he was occupied with a surgical operation. He did, however, arrange for another physician to go to the admissions office. Martha waited on the main floor for the physician—a Negro—to arrive. Suddenly, she felt a presence behind her. It was Louis.

"Come on, let's get out of here," he said gruffly. "I know why you're stalling. You're waiting for the Mafia."

"I'm not waiting for anybody," Martha insisted.

"Yes, you are," he said. "Let's get out of here. I'm going down to the FBI and tell them those people have been following me ever since I left the hotel."

Martha had no other recourse. She went to the Detroit office of the Federal Bureau of Investigation with her husband. There, in the presence of an agent, Louis related the incredible story of his anxiety. While he was talking to the agent, Mrs. Louis went to a telephone and called Smitty. "You'd better come down here," she told Louis's friend. "Joe's telling the FBI all about being gassed and followed by the Mafia."

Within minutes, Smitty was on the scene. A huge man, even taller and heavier than Louis, he handled Joe in the manner of a father talking to his son.

"Come on, Joe," Smitty said, placing his strong right arm around Louis's shoulder. "Let's get out of here. Let's go back to Ford's hospital, pal. They're the people who can help you. You can't get help here."

At first Louis refused, but then relented in the face of Smitty's warm concern. They went to Henry Ford Hospital. This time Louis was quickly checked in. He stayed there for three days while undergoing psychiatric examination. On the third day, Wednesday, he checked out of the hospital.

"You should be here longer," the chief psychiatrist told him.

"Ain't doing me no good here," Louis said. The next day, accompanied by Martha, he was off on another refereeing tour.

Mrs. Louis knew that Louis would not eat unless she prepared the food for him in the hotel rooms in which they stayed. So she carried a hot plate and canned soup and canned fruit with her. She even packed some eggs in a tote bag. In addition, her luggage contained plastic dishes and pots and pans. In the morning she would boil eggs for her husband. In the evenings she would prepare hot soup for him and serve it with the type of crackers he liked. She did all this in such a manner as to win his confidence. But in all her travels with Joe, she was never untouched by apprehension. It was even more difficult for him to find peace.

The Louis Family: Joe, Marva, and daughter Jacqueline (above);
Joe, Jr., Jacqueline, and father at Miami Beach in 1951 (below left);
Joe, Jr., and friend in 1964 as freshmen at Boston University (below
right).

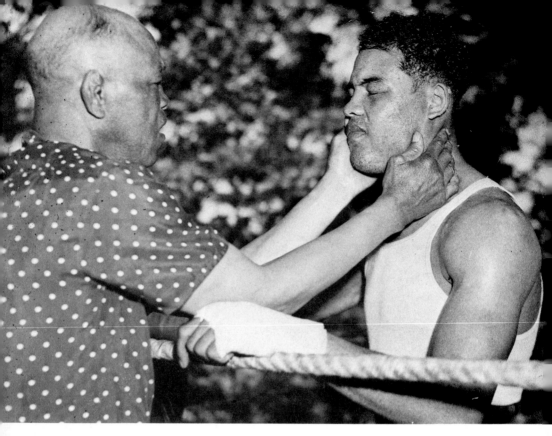

Above, Jack Blackburn with Louis, getting ready for a session with sparring mates. On a boxing tour of South America (below) Joe is shown next to Luis Angel Firpo, "Wild Bull of the Pampas."

In 1942, a day or two after he successfully defended his title against Buddy Baer, Joe Louis entered the army. He is shown on this page at Camp Upton (above right), *visiting wounded soldiers at Fort Devens* (below), *and with four Southampton Island Eskimos during a trip through army bases in the Central Canada command* (above left).

Louis and Billy Conn sign for their 1946 championship fight; Mike Jacobs is leaning behind the champion, boxing commissioner Edward Eagan is at center, and at Eagan's left is Dr. Clilan B. Powell, another boxing commissioner (above). Louis's long-time cook William Bottoms jokes with the champ at training camp shortly before the Conn fight (below right). While her son defends his crown against Conn, Mrs. Lilly Barrow Brooks listens intently to a broadcast of the fight (below left).

Louis flattens Billy Conn in their 1946 championship fight (above). *The Brown Bomber working out with a young admirer* (below right), *and in a publicity photo shortly before his first retirement* (below left).

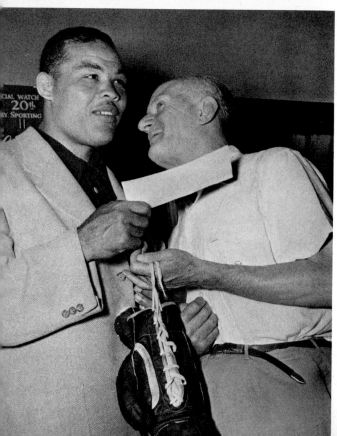

As bodyguard Carl Nelson looks on (above), Joe fends off a young contender. After defeating Joe Walcott in 1948 Louis announced his retirement and symbolically exchanged his gloves for a final check from Mike Jacobs (left).

Louis's public relations firm
contracted to promote tourism
in Cuba. In 1959, Joe and Fidel
Castro were together (below)
at a New Year's party in Havana.
Louis is shown enjoying
his favorite avocation (right).

Joe Louis and wife Martha are shown at a 1971 press conference in New York. The Brown Bomber (below) is honored on his fifty-seventh birthday at Caesars Palace in Las Vegas. Celebrating with him are, left to right, Sugar Ray Robinson, Max Schmeling, Billy Conn, and Gregory Peck.

25

Whenever he speaks of his career in the ring, Louis insists that it was made up of two parts separated by the years he spent in the army. "When I came out of the army I wasn't the fighter I was before I went in," he says. "Nobody can lay off that long and come back as good as he was." This is not hindsight. He knew this back in 1946, and so did the people around him. Immediately after his second fight with Conn, Louis was told by Miles, "Quit now. You shouldn't fight anymore." He thought about the suggestion, but rejected it, though he was aware that there was merit in the recommendation. He found training difficult. Getting up at five in the morning for roadwork was a hardship. And life in a training camp no longer was funny. By the time he was scheduled to fight Jersey Joe Walcott in Madison Square Garden in December 1947, his physical condition was causing alarm among his retinue. He was showing evidence of reflexive deterioration.

Dr. Bennett noticed it first. He would play table tennis with Louis, and when he hit the ball to one side, Louis responded with agility. But when the ball was hit to Louis's other side, the heavyweight champion would react slowly, if at all. Louis's friend and physician talked to Miles.

"Joe is through," he said. "Certain processes are starting. His reflexes are unequal on both sides, and they weren't that way before. I don't think he needs this fight."

"I agree," Miles said, "but I spoke to him about this after the Conn fight. He doesn't want to quit."

Nevertheless, both physician and manager brought up the subject of retirement in their conversations with Louis. He would not be swayed. Finding support for his position in a boxing platitude, he said a fighter wins his championship in the ring and loses it there. He was thirty-three years of age and had defended his championship twenty-three times. Had he resigned his title then the public would have received his decision with understanding and appreciation. He did not comprehend this. Money was greatly on his mind. The prospect of retirement presented the threat of a financial problem that he could not cope with.

Announcement of the fight with Walcott was greeted with derision in the press. Because Walcott's record hardly qualified him for a title fight, Sol Strauss, Jacobs's surrogate, had at first suggested a ten-round exhibition bout. The New York State Athletic Commission rejected the proposal. Once Louis walked into the ring, his championship would be at stake. So the length of the fight was extended to fifteen rounds, the mandatory span of championship bouts in New York State. Louis had not been in the ring for more than a year. Excess weight hampered him. He worked hard to get down to 214 pounds, yet when he stepped on the scale at the formal weighing-in, he was 211 pounds. As in the first fight with Conn, he had dried out—gone off water—too soon before the bout.

Ruby Goldstein, a former lightweight boxer, was the referee. When he had been in the army, Goldstein had accompanied Louis's boxing troupe to Alaska for a series of exhibition bouts, and they had become friends. But Goldstein's reputation for integrity was so widely known, nobody thought it awry that he should be the referee in a fight involving his army buddy. And, after all, Louis had knocked out twenty of his twenty-three challengers. It was a foregone conclusion that he would quickly dispose of Walcott, himself thirty-three years of age. In that case, the referee's vote would have no significance. It did not turn out that way.

Speaking of it later, Louis said, "I don't like to remember that fight. Walcott knocked me down twice, in the first and fourth, and he closed my left eye. I didn't have the strength. I didn't have a punch that night. I was ashamed. When it was over I told Walcott, 'I'm sorry, Joe.' I meant I was sorry it was such a bad fight. I wanted to get out of the ring the minute I heard the last bell. I didn't want to wait for the judges' decision. I got better than $80,000 for that fight, counting movie and radio money, but I never felt so low after a fight. I sat in my Harlem apartment and wondered why I fought so bad. It was worse because the crowd booed when I got the decision. I knew I had to fight Walcott again. I didn't want to retire with that for my last showing."

The way it had turned out, the two judges voted for Louis. Goldstein, Louis's pal, voted for Walcott, whom he awarded seven rounds to Louis's six, with two rounds even.

Hiding away in his apartment was not Louis's customary procedure after a fight. Usually, he would go down to Madison Square Garden the day after a bout to speak with clamorous newspaper reporters. It had been fun. He would walk into promoter Jacobs's office, flop into a large chair upholstered in red leather, and attempt to explain to the reporters what it was all about—the overwhelming desire to win, which justified it all. He would glance at the comic pages, while talking to them, and they would overlook his impoliteness because they knew him to be an absolutely decent person. Inwardly, he found the reporters' questions funnier than the comic pages, but his own sensitivity and inborn decency foreclosed laughter.

Now, in the eleventh year of his time as heavyweight champion, he suddenly felt older. His head had throbbed for hours after Walcott had finished hitting him, and when he looked into a mirror, the image he saw was raw and unfamiliar. He sat in the dark and was worried; until the past few days he had not given any importance to what happened to himself. It was a new and terrible thing; and in the darkened room, he knew suddenly that he was about to make a decision. The next fight with Walcott would be his last. He would definitely retire from the ring.

It was six months before he opposed Walcott again. Two of them were spent in Europe. Miles arranged for Louis to give a series of exhibitions at the Health and Holiday Exposition in Earl's Court in London. Louis was to receive $80,000; and when he sailed for England on the *Queen Mary* in February 1948, he was accompanied by Marva. His retinue included Miles, Seamon, Leonard Reed, Eddie Green, Nelson Sykes, and Irwin Rosee. Reed acted as the court jester, while Green and Sykes went along for the ride. Rosee was Louis's press relations counselor.

The trip was a financial disaster. Instead of receiving $80,000 for the exhibition series in London, Louis eventually was paid $40,000. Sponsors of the exposition went into bankruptcy. But Louis was determined to have some fun. He went to Brussels and then on to Paris. A Swedish promoter got in touch with him to put on a series of exhibition bouts in Scandinavia. Because funds were scarce in Sweden, the promoter offered to pay Louis with ice skates instead of money. The proposal was rejected. In Paris, Louis walked the streets with crowds following him, yelling, "Joe Lou-*ee!* Joe Lou-*ee!*" He was introduced everywhere as "champion le boxe." Hearing this, the thought, acutely painful, came to him: he would have to knock out Walcott to prove that he was really the champion. When he returned to New York on the *Queen Elizabeth*, the fight with Walcott, scheduled for Yankee Stadium on June 24, was little more than two months off. He went into training immediately.

A cloudburst hit Yankee Stadium on the evening of

June 24 and the fight with Walcott was postponed for twenty-four hours. The next night a star-studded blue sky hung over the stadium. Almost 43,000 persons were in the ballpark. Louis, weighing 213 pounds, heard a great shout of adulation when he came into the ring. Walcott's entrance was mildly received by the throng.

Walcott, at 194 pounds, was determined to make the same kind of fight as he had the first time he faced Louis. A counterpuncher, he moved from side to side, straining to force Louis to lead to him. The first two rounds were dull. In the third round, Walcott caught Louis with both hands to the head. Louis went down, but came up so quickly no count was started. They dawdled along, and the throng in the ballpark was overtaken by indifference. In Louis's corner, Seamon exhorted the champion, "Go after him, Joe. He's tiring." By the eighth round, Louis was in command of the battle. He punished Walcott severely with punches to the head. In the ninth, responding to Louis's assault, Walcott withstood them easily and replied with punches thrown in combination. Walcott was defensive in the tenth round, but Louis persisted in his assault. He hurt the challenger. Then, in the eleventh round, the champion's power asserted itself. He hit Walcott with a right to the jaw. Shaken, Walcott retreated. Louis followed him and landed both hands to the head. A smashing right to the jaw put Walcott on the floor. He rolled onto his back. By seven, he had risen to one knee. He was gasping. The referee, Frank Fullam, counted him out. It was Louis's last fight as the heavyweight champion of the world.

Louis's purse of $255,522 did not go directly to him.

Instead, it went to Joe Louis Enterprises, Inc. During the previous December, the corporation had been formed under the direction of Theodore A. Jones, a certified public accountant, and Truman K. Gibson, the Chicago lawyer to whom Louis had appealed in behalf of Jackie Robinson in the Fort Riley incident. Except for one share each held by Jones and Gibson, Louis retained all the stock in the corporation, which took over $115,000 of Louis's liabilities, his contract for personal services, and $5,000 in cash. It would prove to be a vain attempt to straighten out Louis's tangled financial situation.

In the period immediately following Louis's knockout of Walcott, speculation was widespread as to the method Louis would use to resign as world heavyweight champion. The road he chose eventually was constructed by a New Jersey press agent and promoter named Harry Mendel. They had become friends when Mendel had been hired by Jacobs to ballyhoo one of Louis's fights. About Mendel it was once written: "Mendel stood about five feet two inches in silk socks and weighed about 200 pounds. He was a completely extroverted individual who devoured food in huge quantities. When he laughed, which was often, his huge belly shook in rippling rhythm. The effect on Louis was catalytic: the champion would break up in waves of booming laughter. Mendel had learned his way around in speakeasy society and, in earlier times, had worked as a press agent at six-day bike races in Madison Square Garden. He had assumed the role of a warm host whenever he was on a promoter's payroll, and sports writers and columnists flocked around him because of his freewheeling attitude toward pleasure." In this latter regard, Louis also found him attractive.

After the second Walcott bout, Louis went on an exhibition tour organized by Mendel. It covered the South, the eastern seaboard, and the Midwest. The money was rolling in, and Louis was getting rid of it as if it were no longer fashionable.

In Detroit, on his way to box an exhibition bout in Cleveland, Louis encountered his brother Lonny. "I need money," Lonny said.

"We weren't surprised," Miles remembers. "He was always putting the bite on Joe. And, funny thing, Lonny was the only man in the world Joe was physically afraid of. Lonny could threaten him and he would just fold up."

When, on the occasion in Detroit, Lonny asked for money, Joe suddenly stood up to him. "I gave you $30,000 last year," Louis said. His brother moved threateningly toward Joe. He scowled. Then he said, "Yeah, but you didn't give it to me all at one time."

"How much you need?" Joe asked.

"Need seventy-five hundred," Lonny said. "Two checks, one I want to use to buy a bar, the other I need for alimony."

Louis caused two checks to be drawn in favor of his brother, one made out specifically to Lonny, the other in the name of the Domestic Relations Court. The next day, when Louis's troupe arrived in Cleveland, there was a message for him from Detroit: Lonny had cashed both checks by subterfuge and had lost the $7,500 playing blackjack. "He always liked blackjack," Louis said.

Throughout the tour, newspapers frequently printed reports that Louis was about to make formal announcement of his retirement. Strauss, locked in his office in Madison Square Garden, sat in Mike Jacobs's red leather chair and reflected on these reports. Because he discounted Mendel's cunning and Louis's desire to retire, Strauss reached the wrong conclusion.

Strauss truly believed that Jacobs had treated Louis fairly. Hadn't the promoter lent money to Joe whenever he needed it? He did not relate this to a permissiveness ruinous of Louis, but rather to sound business practices. And he himself could remember numerous occasions on which he had demonstrated what he regarded as the 20th Century's allegiance to and affection for Louis. Only recently, he recalled, Joe had come to the Garden and had walked into the boxing club's offices.

"Sit down," Louis told Strauss. "You'd better be sitting for what I'm going to ask."

"I can take it," Strauss said.

"I need some money," Louis said.

"How much?"

Louis raised his right hand with the palm facing Strauss, the fingers extended. He pushed the hand forward three times.

"Oh, you need fifteen hundred dollars," Strauss said.

"No, fifteen thousand," Louis said.

Strauss blanched. "I'll get it for you," he managed to say.

"Can I get it now?"

"Right now."

A check for $15,000 was drawn in Louis's name. "What's it for?" Strauss finally asked.

"Owe a fellow a golf bet," the champion said. "Fellow's waiting for me right now."

Reflecting on this, Strauss could not believe that Louis would turn his back on Jacobs, though he knew fully that his boss's faculties had been severely curbed by the stroke he had suffered. Even while he was thinking of this, Louis's retirement plan was being offered to Gibson by Harry Mendel. It went like this:

1. Joe Louis Enterprises, Inc., would obtain by contract the exclusive services of the leading contenders for the heavyweight championship.

2. Louis would resign as heavyweight champion.

3. Joe Louis Enterprises, Inc., would assign the exclusivity contracts to an individual or corporation willing to pay the price for the right to promote world heavyweight championship bouts.

"I got the guy we can sell this to," Mendel told Gibson. "Jim Norris. He owns the Chicago Stadium and enough stock in Madison Square Garden to choke a horse. He likes boxing. He'll be interested. He's down in Coral Gables. I'll call him."

"Call him," Gibson said.

Mendel phoned Norris the next day and made an appointment to see him—alone. Gibson was furious. Later he would say, "It was Florida, remember, and a fellow didn't like to have Negroes around with him in those days."

In a forty-five-minute conversation, Mendel convinced Norris that the plan would work. "I think what I had better do," Norris said, "is call my partner, Arthur Wirtz, in Chicago, tell him about it, and have him meet with Louis or his representatives; and if he feels the same way as I did about it, then possibly we could make a deal on it."

A deal was made. Louis resigned the championship in a letter to Abe J. Greene, commissioner of the National Boxing Association, a loosely joined organization of state boxing commissions. The letter, obviously composed by Gibson in behalf of Louis, said:

> I learned from your office today that you are in Miami Beach. I am, therefore, writing you there to submit my formal resignation as world heavyweight champion.
>
> I am certain that you know how sorry I must be to let the championship go this way. I have held it for a long time, and I won it in the ring. I expected to lose it the same way I won it. This is the way champions should be made.
>
> However, things have developed so that I think I ought to stick to the decision to retire that I made some time ago.
>
> I would like to thank you, the splendid members of your organization, and the press and public for the fine way they have treated me throughout all the time I was fighting.
>
> I am sending you another letter to tell you in more detail just what I plan to do in the future.

The other letter contained details of the plan to sign up the leading contenders for the heavyweight championship in behalf of Joe Louis Enterprises, Inc. In no time, Greene acknowledged Louis's letters and granted him permission to go ahead with his program.

Shortly thereafter, the deal with Norris and Wirtz was closed. Louis would be paid $150,000 and would become a stockholder in the International Boxing Club, which they would organize for the purpose of promoting a heavyweight championship tournament. Furthermore, Louis would receive $15,000 annually to help in the promotion of boxing generally and the new organization's bouts specifically.

What Louis had done, in effect, was to sell his title. He had often said it should be won and lost in the ring, but when it came to a showdown, he had decided that money was more important than platitudes. For once in his boxing life, he had acted out of a sense of self-preservation. In the end he would see the International Boxing Club destroyed by a federal court's decree declaring it a monopoly. Even before that would happen, he would give up his stock in the corporation. The annual salary of $15,000, a mere financial dribble in terms of the life-style to which he was accustomed, would come to him for a decade. But at that time, March 1, 1949, his retirement had the outward form and substance of a splendid gesture.

Louis's retirement was announced in the old airport terminal at Miami. Norris and Wirtz flanked Louis as he told an assemblage of reporters that he was hanging up his gloves. Wirtz was introduced and so was Greene, who by his presence in his role as commissioner of the National Boxing Association, sanctioned the departure of Louis from the ring and the arrival of the International Boxing Club.

So important was the announcement of Louis's retirement that the usually staid *New York Times* printed it on the front page. Eleven years, eight months, and one week after his coronation and after twenty-five successful defenses, Joe Louis was no longer king of the heavyweights. And he no longer was Mike Jacobs's pawn.

Some months before his resignation, Louis had gone to Miami Beach to see the ailing promoter. They had walked on the beach and pictures of them together had been published in papers throughout the country over captions that spelled out loyalty and long friendship. Nobody knew then that their years together were over.

26

In the latter part of 1969, Louis was finding it more and more difficult to sleep. Even in the Louises' apartment in Los Angeles, he was imprisoned by insecurity. When Martha looks back on that time, she says, "It was pitiful, really. He would tape up all the outlets. He would take a piece of paper and fold it neat and paste it over the grills. That wasn't anything new. What was new was the way he tried to sleep. He would build a cover for the bed. First he would pull the bed over to the dresser and build up a thing and put something at the head of the bed and then take the headboard and put it across. Then he would take another object—like he'd go into our living room and get a big gold-leaf mirror and lay it across everything to weigh it all down. Then he'd take the shade from the window and use it as a backdrop, like the top of a tent. Then he'd crawl up under it in his clothes and lay under it. Only one side of the bed wouldn't be covered, where he'd crawl in. Here he was with his shoes and everything laying under this tent. It was the most pathetic thing in the world.

"Like when Jesse Owens—you know, the Olympic runner—was honored at this hall of fame dinner in Birmingham, Alabama. We went down there for it. We stayed in this hotel, and there was Joe working on this air-conditioning vent, which was quite large. It was so large, Joe could get the upper part of his shoulder up into it after he removed the grill. He had this paper twisted up against the light to make it shine into the vent so he could see. And he said, 'Yeah, this is where they put the stuff up in here. This is where the gas is coming from.' I could have cried.

"And in Florida in February, I guess it was February 1970, I left Joe in Miami and went to Nassau. When I got back the next day, there were grease spots on the ceiling. I said, 'Joe, what on earth is that on the ceiling?' I knew I hadn't seen the spots when I left. It was a brand-new hotel and we were the first ones to occupy the apartment we were in. Joe said, 'I was stopping up the cracks. The poison gas is coming in through them.' I said, 'What do you mean?' He said, 'I got this mayonnaise out of the refrigerator and smeared it over the cracks. They can't get the gas through there.' You know, if it wasn't so tragic I would have laughed.

"The worst thing was that Joe wanted to stay in bed

all day. He didn't have any physical fitness program. At least it would have been more satisfying than what he did. He just ate and slept during the day, and what he ate, I had to push on him. I had to believe there was some solution to all this, but I didn't know where it really lay. Oh, I knew about psychiatric hospitals. Of course I did. And I knew that Dr. Bennett and Dr. Ellison had recommended that course. But Joe wouldn't hear of it, wouldn't even discuss it. Gentle, sweet Joe, I thought—in such trouble. You had to see it to believe it.

"What I really knew about was the 'hold for treatment' law in Colorado. Under it, a person doesn't have to be declared incompetent to be committed to a hospital. I thought about it a great deal. In California a person must commit a violent crime before he can be committed. That wasn't about to happen in Joe's case. I knew that. But I worried. Oh, how I worried. But all I could do was wait."

27

In retirement, the days passed slowly for Louis. There was, ahead of him, no prospect of a large purse to make time pass faster. His debts amounted to $551,312; and while he was not given to worry, he frequently reflected on his unhappy economic position. Of the $551,312, all was owed to the government in back taxes, except $20,896 to Mike Jacobs and $14,000 to Marshall Miles. Louis's total assets were $55,000, including the $10,000 house he had bought for his mother in Detroit, $500 worth of shares in a life insurance company, and an additional $35,000 in shares in the All-American Drink Corporation, manufacturer of Joe Louis Punch, a soft drink. In time, these relatively meager assets were to dwindle to nothing, but even then they appeared insignificant alongside Louis's indebtedness.

The tax indebtedness was largely a product of the purse from the second fight with Conn. He had paid only $115,992 in taxes then, but in 1950 the government had imposed a further assessment of $246,055. Penalties and interest had increased the total to more than $500,000.

The alteration in the taxes had resulted from the government's contention that the return Louis had filed was faulty in two areas. Mike Jacobs's accountant, Nath Ellenbogen, had formulated Louis's tax structure. First, he had claimed exemption for the $66,000 paid to Marva "in lieu of alimony." The government contended this was in error. No deduction would be permitted. Ellenbogen should have indicated the money paid to Marva was "in lieu of alimony *and support.*" The last two words were decisive. Furthermore, the money paid to Jacobs was defined as a business expense and not as a debt. When the government investigated, it found receipts that indicated much of the borrowed money had gone to buy mink coats, diamond rings, and other baubles for Louis's female friends. The item was disallowed. So Louis, now in retirement, was over his head in debt to the income tax people.

He went to see Jim Norris. "I guess I got to fight again," he told the boss of the International Boxing Club. Norris was pleased. Ezzard Charles, an absolutely efficient but colorless heavyweight from Cincinnati, had beaten Walcott in a fifteen-round match promoted by Norris; and the National Boxing Association, in accordance with its agreement with Louis, recognized Charles as the world champion. Nobody else did, and public disinterest was widespread. Norris viewed Louis's need to make a comeback a stroke of luck. He would match the Brown Bomber with Charles on the theory that a victory over Louis would enhance the NBA champion's status. He did not believe that Louis, at the age of thirty-six, could cope with Charles, who was, at twenty-nine, a relatively young man.

Norris summoned Charles's managers, Jake Mintz and Tom Tannas, to a meeting in the Chicago Stadium. He told them about Louis's intention to return to the ring.

"There's one thing," the promoter said, "if you fight him, you can only get twenty percent. He wants thirty-five percent."

"Why? Why?" Mintz screamed. Then, cringing, he stopped talking.

"I don't think it's fair, Jim," Tannas said. "Why does it have to be this way?"

"Because that's the way it is," Norris said.

The fight was scheduled for Yankee Stadium on September 27, 1950. Louis, who had been on an exhibition tour in the South and in Argentina, had no trouble reassembling his training camp staff. Miles was with him and so was Seamon, and it seemed like old times. And there was, in the beginning, the prospect of a large purse. When it was over, Louis's purse came to $100,458, far less than anticipated. The fight drew only 13,562 persons to the stadium, and the proceeds from ticket sales exceeded the $200,000 received for radio and television rights by only $5,370.

Louis's small purse was not the only dreary aspect of the fight with Charles. Louis simply had nothing left in his armory, while Charles, a splendid boxer, hit him almost at will. Louis bled early from facial lacerations, and Charles, respectful of the old and wonderful champion, relented in his assault. After fifteen rounds, the decision went to Charles.

A man who was in Louis's dressing room after the fight later wrote, "The old fighter was a shambling hulk. He was cut above both eyes, one of which was shut tight by swelling. He could not see well enough to pull on his trousers. Friendly hands helped. Sugar Ray Robinson leaned down and put Louis's shoes on for him. The old champion was led out of the stadium by friends."

He had reacted to the fight in his usual graceful way. "I enjoyed the fight and I want to thank you all," he told the sports reporters crowded in his dressing room. "I done the best I can." Then, again, he said, "I'll never fight again."

By November, he was fighting again. He had a series of six fights and won them all. Among these was one with Lee Savold in Madison Square Garden on June 15, 1951. Originally, the bout was to take place at Yankee Stadium two nights earlier; but when it rained, the bout was shifted into the Garden. In his seventeenth year as a professional, Louis could hardly be expected to have the appearance of a fighter in his prime. His head was bald, and his face was puffy. And his gait had been altered by time. Once loose-legged, he now walked stiffly. When he met Savold at midring for instructions from the referee, he appeared huge alongside his rival, who was outweighed by twenty pounds. Louis had no trouble that night because his opponent was as slow on his feet as he was and, consequently, was easy to hit with a jab. Moreover, Louis was able to put together combinations of punches that bestirred memories of the time of his greatness. But he was no longer great, only competent now, and it took him six rounds to catch up to Savold.

In the sixth round, he hit Savold with left hooks to the head and smashing rights under the heart. Savold, weakened by the pace, moved away slowly. Louis pursued him and caught him on the other side of the ring. A wide right landed and was followed by a left hook to Savold's jaw. He went down and rolled over and over, as though he had fallen off a cliff, and the referee counted him out.

Louis had two more fights after the knockout of Savold and won both. He had, people believed, resisted the erosion of time. It made gaffers feel younger, especially those who reflected on time and remembered that seventeen years had passed since Louis had knocked out Primo Carnera in his first fight in New York. Time had endorsed Louis's greatness. He had come on the boxing scene early and had lasted a long time, and his longevity as a hero of the ring was counted in light years. When he should have retired, he could not because he had squandered his share of more than $4 million in purses. And now they were talking about a fight between him and Rocky Marciano, who had never had a professional bout until shortly after Louis's aborted retirement in 1948.

The match with Marciano was signed. Louis would receive forty-five percent of the net receipts. Only fifteen percent would go to Marciano. And the fight was scheduled for Madison Square Garden on October 26, 1951.

Louis went to the old training camp at Pompton

Lakes to train. Doc Bier no longer owned the place, which had been bought by a man named Baumgartner. The old bar where alcohol had been served was gone, and not even the hot-dog stand remained. In this forlorn place, Louis somehow revived the old days, of the time of his greatness. This continuity was derived from his own sense of concept. He had changed, oh! how he had changed. But there still remained a style so basically classic as to shorten the span of time between his first fight with Carnera in New York and the approaching one with Marciano.

Marshall Miles was still associated with Louis, and he went out to Pompton Lakes and managed the camp. Mannie Seamon, who had taken over as trainer after Jack Blackburn's death, worked with Louis. And Leonard Reed was around, acting mostly as Louis's court jester, telling jokes they would later put into an act while performing in night clubs in California and Hawaii. The act didn't do well, Martha Louis would say later, "because it made a fool of Joe, about him being on the floor more than he was on his feet." But at Pompton Lakes, while Louis was training to fight Marciano, he laughed at the jokes and kept his mind off the rigors of training. Because he had been in so many training camps performing the same exercises for almost two decades, boredom was a constant threat.

But he worked diligently and even banged his sparring partners around with punches reminiscent of his old fire. He was extremely confident. He had never been otherwise, and his optimism had been rewarded with victory sixty-nine times out of seventy-one. He went into the ring with Marciano convinced that he could handle his younger, smaller, less experienced, though undefeated, rival.

The fight was scheduled for ten rounds, and in the beginning it appeared as if Louis would last the distance, perhaps win. His jab was working, and he was handling Marciano easily in the clinches. He won at least three of the first five rounds, though Marciano did whack him with a stunning right-hand punch behind the left ear toward the end of the first round. But Louis had shaken it off and had opened slight cuts over Marciano's eyes with his jab in the next few rounds.

Marciano's major weapon was his right, which was thrown overhand and whistled as it went. Because of this, Louis disdained the use of a left hook, which when thrown would have rendered him vulnerable to the overhand right. Then, abruptly, Louis seemed older. In the sixth he moved slower, and Marciano began shoving him around in the clinches. He was being hurt by grazing punches. His legs had deserted him.

Louis took a desperate chance in the closing seconds of the seventh round. He threw the hook, which caught Marciano solidly on the right side of the jaw. The younger man just moved forward disdainfully. By this demonstration of disrespect, he pointed the way to Louis's inevitable defeat.

The end came in the eighth round. It was effected not by Marciano's right hand, but by his left hook. Short and to the point, the hook landed on Louis's head. He went down and took an eight count. When he arose, Marciano pinned him on the ropes and hit him with two more left hooks before launching the last punch of the fight, a right to the jaw that sent Louis through the ropes onto the ring apron, where he lay with only one leg inside the ropes.

Sugar Ray was in a ringside seat. When Louis went down for the first time, he sensed the inevitable conclusion of it all. He began moving toward the ring; and when the end came, he jumped into the ring and consoled Louis, who had fought for the last time.

28

Apart from Martha, the person to whom Louis confided more and more of his fears was a large, dark-eyed friend named Ash Resnick, who runs the casino at Caesars Palace. Around Las Vegas, they were inseparable. They had known each other for years, going back to World War II; and as Resnick was eventually to describe it, their first meeting had been casual. "We both took our physical exams for the army together, on Governors Island. I was playing basketball with the Original Celtics and Joe was the heavyweight champ. The newspapermen took pictures of us together. I didn't see much of Joe during the war, just once in a while. Joe and I became real close, I'd say, about ten years ago, about 1960. I was at the Thunderbird in Las Vegas at that time, running the casino, and Joe used to come over from Los Angeles.

"I was promoting fights in Las Vegas. We had quite a few world championship fights there. Joe was always present at the fights. He was the casino's guest. Joe never lost any money gambling. Whatever money Joe lost in gambling, we gave to him. We knew Joe couldn't win anyway, so it didn't matter. He couldn't win because he doesn't push hard with big bets when he is winning. He was like an unpaid shill for the hotel. I've seen Joe with as much as $6,000 in front of him, and I would tell him, 'Joe, quit. Save the money, put it away.' But Joe wouldn't walk away from the table with the money. He would just keep playing until he didn't have any more. Just as long as he had a dime to get the newspaper and go to sleep, he was happy.

"About three years ago—1967—he began showing signs that he was sick. Anytime we went anyplace, even when Joe had a room in Las Vegas, he would go to his room and take the front of the ventilators off and say that the Mafia was after him, they're putting poison gas in the room. We went to Florida together last year. He had this beautiful apartment all for himself and Martha, at the Carriage House first and then at the Ocean Pavilion. He called me into his room one day and said, 'Ash, see that out in the ocean there. There's a guy in a boat and every night he shines a light into my room.' I said, 'Joe, that's ridiculous.' I knew what was going on. He just got hallucinations.

"I thought if any violence showed up out of them, then there really was something to worry about. But Joe

[182]

was harmless, even though he had these hallucinations. He wasn't hurting anybody. And it didn't seem to mean anything. He was like a kid. He wanted to tape up the ventilators in his room and stuff up the cracks and open the windows wide, so what? He'd say don't turn on the television set, there's poison gas coming out of there. Those were things within himself.

"But I got very much concerned one day in Las Vegas. A friend of Joe's was playing blackjack. Joe was watching him. This guy was playing high stakes and Joe just stood near him, looking over his shoulder. Now there was this other fellow standing behind Joe, looking at the game, an absolute stranger. All of a sudden Joe turned around to the guy and says, 'I know you're following me. You'd better get out of here. I'll knock you right on your ass.'

"Joe had never been violent, never said a mean word to anybody in his whole life. He was like a baby. When we'd be walking around in the street. people would come up to Joe and say, 'Hey, Joe, you remember me? I played golf with you.' It could have been twenty years ago, but Joe would say, 'Oh, yeah, is what's-his-name still the pro there?' He'd remember.

"Right after this thing happened with the fellow who was watching the blackjack game, something else happened. A woman was watching a blackjack game. She was standing near Joe, and he repeated the same thing—that she was following him and that he'd knock her on her ass. I really got concerned, you know, because I felt, God forbid, if any violence showed up in Joe, it was time to do something.

"But I'll tell you, there's not a finer guy than Joe. There's not a finer guy in the whole world. That's what you try to impress on Joe. You know, when he'd say somebody was after him, I'd say, 'Joe, who the hell would be after you? If anybody was after you, they'd have gotten you a long time ago.'

"He blamed Helen Dayton. When he busted up with Helen, he claimed people around her told him to stay away from her or they were going to do something to him. One time, I remember, he called her up on the phone and called her everything under the sun. He told her she was oversexed, and he went back fifteen years and told her things she had done. He said, 'I never want to see you again.' You know, half an hour later he called her to come to Vegas.

"That's how he is. Just unbelievable. You had to know that when you'd see what he'd do with money. I remember once we went to Chicago to a fight. I know Joe had two dollars in his pocket. Some panhandler outside the stadium went over to Joe and said, 'Joe, can you give me a dollar?' Joe gave him two dollars. Didn't have a penny left in his pocket, you know. But he was with me, and it didn't mean anything. But even if he was alone, he just would have given the guy two dollars, too.

"Every time we went somewhere, if we'd get out of a cab or something, Joe would say, 'Give the driver ten dollars, Ash, give him ten dollars.' Only once did I see him act kind of sensible. He had about $6,000 he won at the tables. He sent Martha $2,000. But don't you know, he went back to the tables and lost the other $4,000, or whatever he had left."

[184]

That was Ash Resnick's story. However one looked at it, his position was curious. He was bothered by Louis's problem, but he chose to humor his friend. "It's all a lot of nonsense," he told Joe. But he had to admit to himself that Louis was a very sick man because it was really true.

29

Now retired from boxing, Louis came to know abruptly that he no longer would earn large sums of money for one night of work. He still had the $15,000 annual income from the International Boxing Club, but this was hardly enough to keep him going at the pace he had established for himself when the money was rolling in. He even thought of making a comeback. By then, Jersey Joe Walcott was the world heavyweight champion, having upset Ezzard Charles by a knockout. Walcott was six months older than Louis, and the former champion said, "It's tough to retire when the guy who holds the title is older than you. I've only lost three fights in my life."

In Chicago, Joe Triner, chairman of the Illinois State Athletic Commission, declared that he would not grant Louis a boxer's license. "He should not take chances of being hurt," Triner said. Louis went off on an exhibition tour of the Far East, boxing mostly at U.S. military bases. When he returned on December 20, 1951, the California State Athletic Commission learned that he was contemplating a comeback. Announcement was made that no action would be taken concerning Louis's comeback until he filed an application for a boxer's license. He didn't. The entire issue was forgotten.

Louis spent his time on the golf course. In January 1952 he was invited, as an amateur, to play in the San Diego Invitational Tournament. No sooner had he been invited than he was informed that the Professional Golfers Association had ruled that no black professionals could compete in a PGA-sponsored tourney. Two of Louis's pals, Eural Clark and Bill Spiller, were barred, although one of them, Spiller, actually had qualified. Louis reacted out of character. He made noise. "Getting those fellows in," he said, "is going to be the biggest battle of my life. I want the people to know what the PGA is. We've got another Hitler to get by."

The tournament was cosponsored by Chevrolet dealers in the San Diego area. Nervously, a spokesman for the auto merchants insisted, "We are most anxious that Joe, one of America's true sportsmen, plays in our event." Joe consented to play, even while vowing publicly to fight "racial prejudice in golf, the last sport in which you still find it." In any event, he was the first black to play in a PGA-sponsored tournament. Years later, the ban against blacks was lifted. He would not take sole credit for the change. It had happened in the course of the black man's battle for a kinetic role in a white society. But the first blow had been struck by Louis. He had lost a fortune trying to prove his skill on the links, and in the end, only his contribution to the black cause in this area of sports remains as a monument to his devotion to the game.

He was active in other sociopolitical areas. In Washington in October 1952, he announced that he had always voted Republican but had altered his stance in connection with the presidential race between General Dwight D. Eisenhower and Adlai Stevenson. "I just came back from a trip to the South," he said, "and General Eisenhower's conduct down there is not very good for the black man. The general is running two types of campaigns—one for the South and one for the North, and that doesn't work in the White House in Washington, D.C."

A few days later he turned up at Stevenson's home in Springfield, Illinois. He posed for pictures with the Democratic candidate. One showed him raising Stevenson's right hand. "I'm trying to show him how to throw his Sunday punch," Louis said. To which Stevenson responded, "That might not be a bad idea, Joe." Louis had infrequently selected a winner before an important bout. Indeed, he was a notorious failure as a boxing prognosticator. In politics, he ran to form. When Eisenhower defeated Stevenson, his friends japed at him. "Can't win 'em all," he said.

He was a partner in a public relations agency run by Billy Rowe. They had first established the company in 1946, just before Louis's second bout with Conn. Mike

Jacobs gave them their start. "I'll tell you," Jacobs told
Rowe. "You can work on the fight, doing publicity in
Negro papers from Conn's camp. If the fight does $2
million, I'll give you $10,000. If it don't, you get $5,000."
The fight grossed $74,446 less than $2 million. Jacobs kept
his word. He gave Rowe $5,000.

The business proved more durable than profitable for
Louis. It is still in existence on West Fifty-seventh Street
in Manhattan. But Louis has never really drawn a large
sum from it.

"I've made some contracts for him where he's got
some money," Rowe says. "I've made other contracts
where he hasn't gotten anything, like we did *The Joe Louis
Story*, the moving picture."

The unimaginatively titled *Joe Louis Story* was produced in 1953. It cost $400,000 to make. Of this sum,
Rowe invested $15,000 of his own money. Louis con-
tributed the rights to his biography. Other investors included Walter Chrysler, the auto magnate. Though the
critic for *The New York Times* treated it kindly in an
eight-paragraph review the picture failed to produce a
profit. Insofar as Louis was concerned, it added up to just
another financial flop.

Six weeks after the picture opened in New York,
Louis received a phone call from Detroit. His mother had
suffered a heart attack. He hurried to her bedside. Two
days later, Mrs. Lillie Barrow Brooks was dead. Joe went
to her funeral and cried. Six years later, in the course of
the government's efforts to collect Louis's tax indebtedness of $1,250,000, he agreed to give up his share in his
mother's $5,500 estate. It came to $667.

30

The possibility that her husband was using cocaine was constantly on Martha's mind. When she reflected on this, never with indifference, she often recalled a conversation that they had had in Las Vegas one afternoon. They had been sitting at a hotel bar when they were joined by a prostitute who knew her way around. They talked for a while; and when the subject of illicit drugs came up, Martha seized upon it as a possible key to Louis's secret.

"There must be a lot of show business people on drugs," Martha suggested.

Louis named a singer who had been hooked on narcotics. Then, adding to the list of addicts he had known, he said, "You know how most of them got hooked. They were going around with somebody, or fooling around with them, and they got shown how to use the stuff."

"You seem to know a lot about it," Martha said.

Without pause, Louis went on. "Some of them people even got hooked while they were sleeping. They didn't even know they were getting it."

Martha pursued the conversation. She questioned Louis about his own implied involvement. She asked, "Joe, you wouldn't be a big enough fool to get hooked if somebody gave you narcotics."

"I don't know what I'd do," he said.

"You don't know what you'd do?" she said angrily. "You got to be kiddin'."

End of conversation.

By then, Louis was, in Martha's words, "taping up holes, knocking on other people's doors, doing all kinds of crazy things like figuring somebody was shooting gas in on him."

She was terrified when Louis told her one day that a woman he knew had described to him the effects of an LSD trip.

"What did she say?" Martha asked.

"She said it was beautiful." Louis said.

"Didn't the acid hurt her? I understand it affects the brain."

"No, she's okay," Louis said.

"I hope you wouldn't be fool enough to let somebody talk you into using LSD," she said.

"I ain't dumb," Louis said. "I wouldn't do that."

[191]

But Martha continued to worry. And she kept her eyes and ears open. In pursuit of information, she invited a woman to visit her in her room. "I didn't think the ordinary layman looking at Joe and seeing him play crap and blackjack and talking would be able to have any insight into Joe's problem," she told an acquaintance later. "And knowing that this woman was in on the know out there with all those drug people, I felt it would hit home to her if she really saw the way Joe's room was. It would give her an idea of his condition, would hit her between the eyes."

The woman took one look at the room and expressed astonishment. The grills on the air-conditioning outlets had been taped over. Louis had removed the mattress from his bed and had placed it on the floor, where he believed he was safer from imagined poison gas.

"I really didn't know Joe was in this bad shape," the visitor said.

"Of course he is. That's the reason I invited you up here."

"One thing I can tell you, I don't know about anything else, but Joe hasn't used LSD. He did mention something to me about red devils. But he never took them either."

"Red devils?" Martha asked.

"It's really Seconal, a barbiturate," the visitor explained. "It just puts you on the nod."

When they left the room together, Martha Louis was satisfied that her husband had used neither acid nor red devils. She was not as reassured about cocaine.

31

March 16, 1956, Washington, D.C. The opportunity to see Joe Louis in action had drawn 4,100 persons to the Uline Arena. They had come not to see him box, but to witness the former world heavyweight champion's debut as a wrestler, a form of show business looked down upon even by the tricky people who populated the world of boxing. "Ain't you a little ashamed of being a wrestler?" somebody asked Louis. He replied, "Beats stealing, don't it?" and the subject was dropped. So was Louis's opponent, a 320-pound former cowboy called Rocky Lee. After ten minutes of wrestling, during which Lee held Louis in his grasp most of the time, the referee, Jersey Joe Walcott, pulled the former cowboy off Louis's neck. Louis spun Lee around and hit him on the jaw with his right forearm, an illegal blow in boxing but perfectly acceptable in the wrestling ring. The cowboy collapsed and was counted out.

Some time later, while on tour with Lee, Louis went into the ring with him in Columbus, Ohio. Louis's obese opponent tossed him to the canvas. Looking up at Lee, Joe expected the erstwhile cowboy to seize him in a headlock. Instead, Lee jumped upon Louis. His feet landed on Louis's left side, crushing several ribs, causing a cardiac contusion. After a short period of convalescence, Louis, spurred by a need for funds, applied for a wrestling license in Chicago. He was forty-two years of age and in less than perfect condition. An electrocardiogram was taken. It disclosed a cardiac abnormality. "He's going to have to rest for the present," said Dr. Irving Slott, a physician for the Illinois State Athletic Commission. Louis's career as a wrestler was finished. A lucrative source of revenue was closed off.

There were other disturbing notes that year. The government filed two more liens against Louis, bringing his tax indebtedness to $1,243,097. And, furthermore, the government proceeded to institute action to seize two trust funds set up in 1947 and 1949 for Jacqueline and Punchy. The funds amounted to $65,688, with the portion allotted to Punchy roughly $4,000 more than Jacqueline's share. The case, heard in a federal tax court, resulted in a decision in favor of the government, based upon the contention that when Marva had established the trust funds, she had used money her husband owed the government in taxes. One year later, a federal appeals court upheld the verdict.

Louis's main source of income still came from the International Boxing Club. His annual salary had been raised from $15,000 to $20,000. But the IBC was in trouble. On June 24, 1957, Judge Sylvester J. Ryan of the United States District Court, Southern District of New York, ordered the boxing club dissolved, declaring it a monopoly in the promotion of professional championship boxing contests in violation of the Sherman Act. Eighteen months would pass before Judge Ryan's decision would be sustained by the Unites States Supreme Court. The organization founded as a direct result of Louis's sale of the heavyweight title to Jim Norris for $150,000 was no longer in existence. In its place Norris organized National Boxing Enterprises, with headquarters at the Chicago Stadium. Louis was retained as an employee of the new company at the same annual salary of $20,000. When he married Martha Malone Jefferson a month later, this was the major source of his income.

He had been an original stockholder in the International Boxing Club and had been promised a share of the profits. He had never collected a cent. And when the successor company, National Boxing Enterprises, went out of business, his $20,000 salary went with it. Martha Louis's husband was out of work.

32

The style of Louis's life was not altered by the loss of his $20,000-a-year job. Martha's law practice was thriving, and they lived in a ten-room house in Los Angeles in which she had installed nine television sets. One of the sets was placed in the bathroom at such an angle that Louis could see it through a strategically placed mirror even when he was taking a shower. When he was not at home looking at television, he was playing golf. Frequently, he would play in Las Vegas, where he would be Ash Resnick's guest at the Thunderbird. His only business interests were with the Louis–Rowe public relations firm in New York.

The year before, the firm had become involved in a public relations deal with the Fidel Castro government in Cuba, and it had caused Louis some embarrassment. In exchange for an annual fee of $25,000, plus fifteen percent of a $262,000 yearly budget for advertising and promotion, the company was obliged to present Cuba as an "unbiased, open-hearted section of Latin America" to which black Americans could go for their vacations. The contract was held in the name of Louis, Rowe, Fisher, Lockhart Enterprises. Louis was listed as a vice-president, while the actual contract with Cuba's National Institute of Tourism had been signed by Maurice Alvin Lockhart, second vice-president of the company.

On New Year's Eve of 1960, Louis and Martha were in Havana as guests of the Cuban government. She was uneasy. During the past few days, she had known an anxiety that was new to her. She told Joe, "I have a funny feeling Castro has communistic leanings. You shouldn't be involved in this."

"It's just a publicity account," Joe said. "They just want our people to come down here for their vacations."

"Oh, yeah, our people have enough money to do that? Don't be a fool, Joe."

Nevertheless, on New Year's Eve she went with Louis to a banquet at the Havana Hilton Hotel. Martha sat at Castro's left at the head table. It was a lively evening, with the guests straining to get Castro's autograph, but Martha's sense of anxiety was not interrupted by the gaiety.

Shortly after their return home, Louis seemed restless. He said, "I've got to go on a trip with Bill Graham."

[197]

She smiled. "I guess," she said, "it's another one of those million-dollar deals that never pan out." Louis said, "Bill's a good friend. He's always trying to do something for me."

Some days later, Martha's intuition told her that Louis was about to return to Cuba. She phoned him in New York. "I understand you got to go to Cuba," she said. He insisted this was not the case. "Oh, no, no, no, I'm not going," he said. "I'm coming home." He gave her the number of his flight from New York.

On the morning of his scheduled arrival, Martha was trying a case at Juvenile Hall in Los Angeles. She rushed through the business at hand and then drove to the airport to pick up Louis. He wasn't on the plane. When she got home, a telegram from her husband informed her that he was on his way to Detroit. She waited for further word. None was forthcoming. So that evening, she telephoned Havana. Joe was there.

"So you're in Detroit," she said. "Beautiful."

He stammered a meaningless reply.

"How long you going to be there?"

"Two or three days."

"Oh, two or three days," she said. The softness of her manner masked her anger. She said good-bye and hung up.

Then, waiting a few minutes, she called back. This time she asked for Miss Dayton's room. Louis himself answered the phone.

"Oh, so Miss Dayton's down there too," Martha said.

"She came down here to get some sunshine," Louis replied against a background of laughter.

"That's a beautiful story, Joe," Martha said. "Why couldn't you tell me originally that you were going to Cuba? And I want you to know I couldn't care less about Helen. Tell her that."

That was all. A week or so later, Louis was back in Los Angeles. Martha told him off. "You think this Cuba business is a plaything," she warned him. "It's not over yet."

When Floyd Patterson went into training some months later for his second bout with Ingemar Johansson, the promoters of the world heavyweight championship fight hired Louis to help ballyhoo the event, scheduled for the Polo Grounds on June 20, 1960.

Three weeks before the fight, the story of Louis's association with Castro broke in the papers. Billy Rowe, as president of the public relations company, attempted to justify the deal. No, Louis had not registered with the Department of Justice as a foreign agent. The company had. "Mr. Louis is disassociated from this account," Rowe said, "and Mr. Lockhart is account supervisor. Certainly, there is nothing political about it. Any implications that there is is completely erroneous. We have no feelings about Cuba's political life and were not hired to do that." Rowe acknowledged that the company had received $52,-934, including a quarterly payment of $6,250 on the annual fee.

Immediately, the promoters of the Patterson–Johansson fight informed Louis that his services were no longer required. They feared that even his tenuous connection with Castro would hamper the sale of tickets for the bout.

Martha reacted quickly. She caused a press conference to be called at the Hotel Commodore in New York. "I have been accused of working for Castro," Joe said. "I've been accused of selling out my country. The only thing I can do is what I'm going to do." He announced that he would divest himself of any interest in the public relations firm unless the contract with Cuba's National Institute of Tourism was permitted to lapse. "It is a matter of principle," Martha said.

Rowe was in Mexico on vacation. Joe sent him a telegram. "Why don't we pull out, let's not wait," Louis urged Rowe, who rushed back to New York. He told Joe, "You know, we've got a lot of money tied up in the contract, money for advertising we laid out and haven't received payment for from Cuba." Without hesitation, Louis said, "The hell with it."

Five weeks later, Rowe's company informed the Cuban government that the contract was no longer in force. "We are Americans first," Rowe said. The company lost money on the deal. Louis's share of the losses came to $1,500.

The last big money Louis had made was the $100,000 he had been guaranteed for his wrestling tour back in 1956. Martha knew there was a need to find something for him to do, to uncover a new source of revenue, and to keep him busy. By February 17, 1962, over much opposition from a Los Angeles promoter named Aileen Eaton, Martha obtained for Louis a license to promote boxing in Los Angeles.

"It wasn't easy," Martha said subsequently. "You would have thought, with all the love the world is supposed to have for Joe, that he would be welcomed as a promoter. But Aileen Eaton eyed her own role as promoter with great pride and wanted to keep out any rival promoters."

It would have been better for the Louises if Mrs. Eaton had succeeded in her effort to block Joe from establishing the United World Enterprise, Inc., his promotional company. Within one year, losses amounted to $30,000. Louis simply paid the fighters more money than the going rate. When Martha protested, he said, "I was a fighter. I know how tough it is. Pay them good." The company went out of business.

"It was my money," Martha told a friend. "But it went the way of the board like most of Joe's enterprises. You know, I often think of this. The most kept-alive thing that bears Joe Louis's name is the milk company in Chicago that sells 'Joe Louis Milk.' And, of course, this hasn't been done through Joe's efforts because he doesn't have any active interest. Jesse Thornton and Helen Thornton started it. Now she's his widow—married to George Jones, who is quite an active businessman—and she carries it on quite successfully. Joe sold the use of his name outright. But, like I said, it's kind of an asset. It puts Joe's name in with a successful business."

33

Through the early sixties, Louis was quite content to exist inside a drifting life. He went where the tide took him, picking up fees as a wrestling referee or for an occasional testimonial. But his earning capacity was far from spectacular. One year his income dropped to $10,-000. He was, by then, "current" with his income taxes, which meant that he was paying only on money earned at the time. Early in the decade, Dana Latham, the Internal Revenue commissioner, had established a policy toward Louis. Latham told Congress, "We have gotten all we could possibly get from Mr. Louis, leaving him with some hope that he can live. He cannot make any large amount of money. His earning days are over. We did not get by any manner or means what he owed us."

But the government's attitude toward Louis's tax situation vacillated, depending for its viewpoint on the man in charge of income taxes in Washington, a circumstance that caused him some woe when he went to work with Pearl Bailey, the singer, at the Riviera in Las Vegas in July 1965. Miss Bailey was paid $35,000. Of this sum she agreed to pay Louis $4,000 to exchange a few quips with her on the stage. The government stepped in and insisted it would take $3,500 of Joe's money on the "old" taxes, leaving him with only $500.

Martha, in her dual capacity as Louis's wife and lawyer, went to Washington and discussed the matter with the income tax authorities. She told them, "It would be no advantage to Joe to work if you are going to take this attitude. He might as well sit down." Martha established her point. Louis was taxed on his estimated income for the year and not as a tax debtor who owed the United States of America more than $1,250,000.

Some time later, he went to London to work as a host at a gambling club in Piccadilly called the Pigalle Sporting Club. All his expenses were paid by the management. While in London, he flew to Frankfurt to see Muhammad Ali defend the world heavyweight championship against Karl Mildenberger. Everywhere he walked, he drew large crowds. The fans yelled, in German, "The Brown Bomber! The Brown Bomber!" It was like old times for him.

One day he flew to West Berlin and toured the Wall, accompanied by a television crew from the Columbia Broadcasting System. "Harlem looks better," he said.

Then, entering through Checkpoint Charley, he was in East Berlin. The TV director asked him to pose for an interview in front of a memorial to Soviet soldiers slain in the Battle of Berlin. Cameras were set up, but just as the interview was about to begin, a short, round policeman arrived on the scene.

"Verboten! Verboten!" he screamed.

"It is the Brown Bomber," an American said.

The policeman took a long look at Louis. Recognizing him, he screeched, "Der Braune Bomber! Der Braune Bomber!" He scurried away, only to return within minutes with a dog-eared paperback picture biography of Louis. Thrusting the book into Louis's hands, he asked Joe to autograph it. Louis turned the worn, yellow pages until he came to a fuzzy picture of his knockout of Schmeling. He chose that page on which to inscribe his signature. The interview went on.

In Frankfurt, Louis stayed at the Intercontinental Hotel. An hour or so after Muhammad Ali had knocked out Mildenberger in the twelfth round, a group of Americans was seated in the dining room of the Intercontinental. Among them was Jimmy Brown. Acclaimed as the greatest running back in the history of professional football, the former Cleveland Browns star had lately undertaken a new career in Hollywood.

Before long, the conversation around the table turned to Louis, who was not present. Because of Muhammad Ali's role as a black activist, an inevitable comparison was made between his militant attitude and Louis's philosophical stand on the black man's struggle for justice.

"In his time, Louis did as much for the black cause as Muhammad Ali," somebody said.

"I don't buy that," Brown said. "You like Louis because he's the kind of Negro you want him to be. He could have been, should have been, more outspoken on the problems of blacks."

Brown said this with a measure of asperity in his voice. Tempers flared. For a moment it appeared that the debate would get out of hand, though nobody in his right mind would dare challenge the awesomely constructed Brown physically. At that moment, Louis came into the restaurant and sauntered toward the table occupied by the Americans.

He was in a happy humor and his face, lit by a broad smile, appeared especially attractive. Brown rose from his seat, threw his huge arms around Louis and said, "Joe, it's so good to see you." Louis responded in much the same manner. When Louis sat down, the conversation concerned itself with Muhammad Ali's remarkable ability as a fighter.

The next day Louis was back in London, where he was joined by his friend Robby Margolies, Abe's brother. Robby had been instrumental in putting Louis to work at the Pigalle. Together, they toured London. Once, while they were getting out of a cab, Louis said, "Robby, give the driver a good tip." To which Robby replied, "Why don't you tip him?" Louis reached into his pocket, pulled out a ten-pound note and handed it to the cabbie. "That's a good tip," he said.

"Do you know how much you gave him?" Robbie demanded. "That was twenty-eight dollars."

"No kiddin'," Louis said.

It was Robby Margolies's custom to bet on fights; and when Floyd Patterson came to London to box an English greengrocer named Henry Cooper, he asked Louis, "Who's going to win?" Without hesitation, Louis said, "Cooper. Patterson can't stand up." Immediately, Margolies put a 1,000-pound bet on Patterson.

When Patterson knocked out Cooper in four rounds, Louis and Margolies were at ringside. "I'm sorry I gave you a bum steer," Louis said. Margolies laughed. "You don't think I'd go along with you," Margolies said. "I got a thousand pounds down on Patterson at 7 to 5. You've got half my bet." Louis's reputation as a fallible prognosticator of fights had brought him a windfall.

There was another windfall in London. When Louis had been there in 1948, he had left some $5,000 in pound notes in a safety-deposit box in a bank near Piccadilly Circus. He left London without clearing out the box, and later he lost the key to the vault.

"If I ever get back there," he had told Martha, "I'll get that money."

"How can you get it if you don't remember the bank?"

"When I get to Piccadilly Circus, I'll find my way," he said. "I'll remember."

Near Piccadilly Circus, Louis found a branch of Barclay's Bank. He went in and told the branch manager his extraordinary story. The bank's records were checked and indicated that Louis indeed had owned a safety-deposit box there in 1948. When he had not claimed its contents after a number of years, the box had been opened and the money found therein put on deposit for him. He came home from London a richer man.

34

During the time Louis was developing symptoms of his paranoia, he wavered between sweat-drenched sleep and half-awake fantasy. The recurrent theme was centered always on Helen Dayton and a plot to involve him in the making of pornographic films. Martha became a phantom character in his hallucinations. Somehow, he believed, she was part of the Mafia's conspiracy to murder him. He was constantly on the move. For long periods of time his haven would be the Louises' Los Angeles apartment, to which they had moved after Martha had sold their ten-room house. Then, driven compulsively, he would take off either for Las Vegas or New York.

In New York he would work on a fee basis for the National Maritime Union. Bill Perry, a vice-president of the organization, had introduced a boxing program in the union hall; and Louis, vaguely associated with this endeavor, concerned himself mostly with spreading goodwill among members of the union. His mere presence was noisily recognized by the black membership as a token of good tidings. He would shake hands all around and sign autographs; and in this genial way he fulfilled his obligation to spread tranquillity among the membership, though he himself was being driven by inner demons.

In the midst of all this there was another cause for disquietude. The source of this problem was physical—a diseased gall bladder. Louis went to Detroit, where Dr. Bennett examined him and recommended surgery. When the gall bladder was removed, it was found to contain five stones. Within a few days, Louis was sitting up in bed in Kirwood Hospital. He was cheery and submitted to interviews by newsmen. Forthrightly, he asserted that Muhammad Ali had made a mistake by refusing to serve in the army, an opinion with which the Supreme Court would disagree three years later. "But that army business doesn't mean he ain't the champion," Louis said. "Nobody's got a right to take that away from him until he goes to jail or retires."

When Louis came out of the hospital, Richard Nixon and Hubert Humphrey were locked in a one-on-one battle for the presidency. Aware of Louis's influence in the black community, each side sought his endorsement. Along the way he indicated he would support the Republican candidate. Perry confronted him. "How can you do that, Joe?"

Perry demanded. "We're supporting Humphrey, and we're paying you. It don't look good for us." Louis offered no argument. "I'll switch," he said.

One night in July 1968, Louis turned up at a national Humphrey-for-President Committee dinner at the Waldorf Astoria. He stood on the dais with the Democratic candidate and thereby acknowledged his support of Humphrey. "It wasn't his conviction," Martha said some time afterward. "I think Joe, whoever he likes at the moment without any concern about political affiliations, goes for that man."

In Las Vegas, Ash Resnick told Louis, "That Humphrey was dead the minute you came out for him. You ain't picked a winner in twenty years." Louis, as always, laughed at himself. He could not know then that when the time would come for him to be delivered to a psychiatric hospital, he would, in a fruitless gesture, turn to President Nixon for help.

35

Martha Louis could wait no longer. The hallucinations, delusions, and false perceptions suffered by her husband made life intolerable for both of them. She had to act quickly; and while in Denver early in 1970, she discovered much to her relief that the state of Colorado had in 1963 amended its statutes regarding the mentally sick to permit the very kind of treatment Joe needed. The law granted the probate court the authority to commit a person to a psychiatric hospital for a period of three months for observation, diagnosis, and treatment. Furthermore, this could be done without a preliminary hearing. How fortuitous had been her purchase of the house in Denver.

It had come about in 1964 when she was retained by Sonny Liston, then the world heavyweight champion, to act as his attorney in connection with his first bout with Muhammad Ali, which was held in Miami Beach. Liston lived in Denver at the time; and when she had gone there to discuss legal matters with him, she had come to like the city. She decided to buy a home there. Now, facing a difficult decision, she found the answer in Denver.

There was only one drawback. When Louis was taken to the Colorado Psychiatric Hospital, he was advised that the law gave him the right to a hearing before the "court or before a medical commission . . . at any time that the order to hospitalize is in effect." Before his transfer to the Veterans Administration Hospital from the Colorado Psychiatric Hospital, Louis had insisted on such a hearing. The outcome of the appeals process was predictable. Louis was a sick man. By the time he had switched hospitals, it was apparent that more extensive evaluation would be needed to make an exact psychiatric diagnosis. An agreement was reached. Louis would forego his right to a hearing; he would remain in the hospital.

The Veterans Administration Hospital in Denver is at 1055 Clermont Street, adjacent to a complex of buildings housing, among other institutions, the University of Colorado Medical School and the Colorado Psychiatric Hospital. It is an eight-story building without exterior distinction—red brick, a shallow lawn surrounding it on four sides, a long cement walk leading to a lobby with the usual terrazzo floor and decorative pilaster columns set against the walls. In a corridor off the lobby a bank of elevators moves staff, visitors, and ambulatory patients to the upper floors. The first time Louis ascended to the seventh-floor psychiatric ward, he was apprehensive. He was assigned to a private room next to an office used by one of the hospital staff.

"Can't sleep there," he told Martha. "See that office next door, that's being used by the people after me. I think the hospital is in on it."

"Don't be silly, Joe," Martha said.

"They're all in on it. They're gassing the hospital. They're putting the air down from the eighth floor."

"Why don't you move?" Martha suggested.

"They're everywhere I go. They got a thing they can see me anywhere I go."

"They must have some high-powered equipment," Martha said.

"They see right through the walls," Louis said. "put the stuff right through the brick walls."

Sleep mostly eluded him. Instead of using his own bed, he narrowed his world to the reading room, where there was a television set, and to the treatment room, where he would climb up on an examination table with his clothes on. There, numbed by a sense of desolation, he sought sleep. It came intermittently. In his alternate retreat, the reading room, he would put two chairs together and recline on them. In this way he might sleep for a few hours.

Dr. Martin, the ward chief, prescribed "rather high doses" of Thorazine, a major tranquilizer and psychotropic drug widely used in state hospitals throughout the country. It decreases anxiety and excitement and restores a patient to rational thinking. Louis was given the drug four times each day: twice before noon, once in the late afternoon, and just before bedtime. In addition, he took Hydrodiuril, a diuretic, each morning to control his high blood pressure, which had been 180/120 when he was admitted to the hospital.

Twice a week, usually on Monday and Friday, Louis met privately with Dr. Martin, his therapist. He would recount his "long, complicated, incredibly detailed" irrational story involving "a number of individuals, principally his wife and a mistress by the name of Helen. At about the time his story started, he had apparently begun using cocaine on occasion to make him 'more relaxed and self-confident.' "

Dr. Martin won Louis's confidence. "He's the only one around the hospital that knows what he's doing," Joe would say later. And in a matter of months Dr. Martin would write of Louis, "He received individual as well as group, occupational, and recreational therapy. The patient was quite suspicious, anxious, and distrustful early in his hospitalization. This therapist was very honest and open with the patient in their relationship and made every effort to avoid becoming involved in the patient's delusional system. This attempt continued to be successful and to that extent the patient developed a trusting and open relationship with the therapist."

Louis was extremely popular in the ward. He expressed himself freely in the group therapy sessions and listened carefully to the stories of other patients.

"They talk a lot about suicide," Louis told a visitor. "But I think ninety percent of them think about getting back home with the families and back into life. And then you get some talking about suicide. I make comment about this suicide talk when I talk to them, when they talk, tell their story, you know. I tell each one, talk them out of the idea of trying suicide, give them hope that they will be back with their family. I have a lot of discussions about that.

"We had one woman on the ward that thought about it quite frequently. She's discharged now. And we had another boy who had both legs taken off—wasn't taken off—paralyzed from the waist down. No, he got hit when he got out of combat. He turned over in a jeep. He spoke about it quite frequently. I used to tell him all the time—he liked guns—that it don't pay to shoot himself.

"We meet in a large group and know each other's story. Then we break up in small groups; so the small groups talk about their problems. Or if something is gone wrong in the ward, we have a meeting we call a community meeting, when we talk about the ward, about what's going on in the ward, that a certain patient ain't taking care of his responsibility on the ward. They don't keep the ward clean, throw cigarettes on the floor, don't clean up the bathroom, go in, use the bathroom, usually flush it, but a lot of time they leave it standing right there in the thing. So, of course, we talk about it, and the ones that do it are mostly patients that are pretty sick. They're on heavy medication, see, so they don't know what they're doing all the time.

"We have a rule that we made up among the patients and the doctors. If you have a group meeting and you miss the meeting, you go on restriction. Restriction mean you got to stay on the ward. You can't come downstairs, walk through the hallway, go and get no fresh air or go visiting.

I've been on restriction. Only twenty-four hours. In fact, the first time they put it in, I missed a 1:30 meeting. I had to meet my wife down near the putting course back of the hospital. I forgot about the meeting. That's the main reason I wasn't there.

"We had this girl on the ward that wanted a newspaper yesterday. I bought it for her and put it on a chair for her. Another patient come by and took it. When she found out, she hit the fellow. We talked about it in our group. I told her it was wrong to hit anybody."

36

Louis often reflected on his situation. Suppose Punchy had not signed the application for his commitment, would he be in the hospital? He knew Martha could have signed in his son's place. But the thought that Punchy had done the deed bothered him. "He ain't been around me," the father said of his son. "How come he sign? He didn't know what I was doing. She did."

But when he was given a pass to spend a weekend at home, he immediately telephoned to make an appointment to play golf with Punchy on Saturday. Martha was not at home. She had gone to Detroit on business. Neither was Punchy there. Louis did not know that Punchy was serving two weeks of active duty with the National Guard. The phone was answered by a girl who was staying at the house during Martha's absence. She, too, was unfamiliar with the situation. "I'll tell Punchy about it," she said. The message was never delivered.

Dr. Martin asked Louis, "Did you get in touch with your son?" Louis said, "I talked to him at the bank." This was not true; Punchy had not been for two weeks at the bank in which he worked. So Dr. Martin was mistakenly assured that Louis would not be at home alone over the weekend.

Louis, looking forward to a round of golf with his son, arrived at home to find nobody there. Angered, he picked up his golf clubs and went to the course himself. That evening, Punchy returned from National Guard duty. He was surprised that his father was home from the hospital.

"They shouldn't let you out when nobody's here," the young man told his father.

"You knew I was coming. I called."

"I didn't get the message. I wasn't home."

The disturbing conversation ended. Louis told Martha, "When I get back to the hospital, I'm taking that boy's name off the visiting list." He did not carry out his threat.

Martha visited Louis daily. She would purchase five dollars' worth of fruit for Joe, most of which he would distribute among the patients in Seven North. He was the ward's benefactor. One day, on their way to a visit with Dr. Martin in his office adjacent to the elevators off the seventh-floor ward, Martha saw Joe stop to talk to another patient. Louis reached into his pocket, withdrew a ten-dollar bill, and handed it to the other patient.

"What's that?" Martha asked.

"Nothing, Martha, he's got a pass to go out. I gave him ten dollars. I feel sorry for them people."

Louis had other visitors. Ash Resnick flew over from Las Vegas to see his friend. He found Louis in bed. "Joe was just woozy," he said later. "He could hardly talk. He was just laying in bed and mumbling. It was pitiful. I guess it was the medication. But what was worse was the guy in the next bed, who was saying, 'If I only had the clip to my Luger I would kill those Germans.' He was probably in the war, shell-shocked or something. I couldn't stand seeing Joe in such a place."

Bill Perry visited from New York. "You've got a lot of expenses," he told Martha. "Here's a check for you." She took it. The check was in the amount of $1,000. "It's going to help a lot," Martha told Perry.

One morning, Abe Margolies showed up at the hospital. "I hope you come with some refueling," Louis said to Margolies, who had in the past supplied him with rather large sums of money.

"What do you do with money, Joe?" Margolies asked.

"Lots of poor folks here," Louis said.

Margolies gave Joe $200. "Gonna help a lot of people here," Joe said. "Did you bring the ring I asked for?"

"I got it," Margolies replied. "Who's it for?"

"One of the nurses," Louis said. "I promised it. She's a nice lady."

A young man with a blank stare approached Louis,

who talked to him softly. "He's very sick," Joe told Margolies, who thought, "What a man. He's sick himself and he's thinking of other people."

And other people were thinking of Louis. Each week his mail from well-wishers totaled more than one hundred letters. Some of the letters ran to four hand-written pages. The encouragement they offered exhorted him to fight now as he had fought in the ring. "You're still the champ," one letter said. "You're going to win this fight the way you won all the others." Another came from Henry Armstrong, the only man in boxing to hold three world championships simultaneously. "You always depended too much on friends instead of yourself," Armstrong wrote. "Why not try God now? He will solve your problems."

For several days a stranger attempted to gain admission to Seven North. He said he was from Chicago and represented the Church of Scientology. Somehow, he managed to get in to see Louis, though he obviously was not on the list of accredited visitors. He attempted to recruit Louis, a nominal Baptist, into the Church of Scientology, which claims 6 million adherents and 700 churches throughout the world. In essence he suggested that Louis could defeat self-doubt and mental illness by subscribing to the rules of positive thinking prescribed by L. Ron Hubbard, founding prophet of Scientology. Louis rejected the opportunity for self-analysis. He turned the missionary away.

Martha was furious when she learned of the incident. A day later the Scientologist turned up at her home. "I'm tired tonight," she told him, "come back another time."

The next day was Saturday and Louis, home from the hospital, was in the living room when the Scientologist returned. He spoke again of the wisdom of Scientology. Martha turned on him.

"You've got some nerve going to the hospital and seeing my husband without checking with his doctor, without knowing the background of his illness," Martha said.

"We only want to help," the Scientologist said. "We have helped others. We believe we can help Joe Louis. Just think of what it would mean if we did that. He can begin right now by signing this card."

"Joe's not signing anything," Martha said firmly.

"I don't know whether you want to help your husband," the Scientologist said.

"You didn't have to come out here to find that out," Martha shouted. "All you had to do was to ask anybody who knows us that I've always been for Joe. I've gone through so much for this man, nobody would believe it, not even myself."

New protestations, new justifications were offered by the Scientologist.

Finally, in exasperation, Louis spoke up. "Better go now, man. We ain't signing no cards. You want me to sign so you can show me off. You got a thing going, too. Everybody's got a thing going."

The admonition was heeded. The missionary left. Without giving it a thought, Louis had opted for psychiatry as the source of his inner redemption. On Monday he was back in Seven North.

37

Detroit to Joe Louis: "Welcome Home, Champ," that eight-column headline appearing on the front page of the *Michigan Chronicle*, a black newspaper, posed a problem for Louis. It presumed that the former champion would be in Detroit on August 12 to accept the plaudits of some 8,000 persons assembled in Cobo Hall, the city's convention center.

The moving force behind the testimonial to Louis was Miss Rosa Owens, a diminutive black woman who ran the Bright Life, an after-care private institution for mentally disturbed persons. A year or so before his own commitment in Denver, Louis had visited Miss Owens's place.

"He was such a boost to the morale of the patients," she said afterward, "I thought what a wonderful thing it would be for Detroit to honor this man who has done so much for others."

A committee was formed to organize the event. It included many black community leaders who formulated as their goal the establishment of a fund to defray any medical costs Louis might have if he were to enter a private hospital. A program of entertainment was arranged. In Lansing, the state capital, Governor William G. Milliken issued a proclamation.

Thirty-three years ago on June 22, 1937, Joe Louis became the Heavyweight Champion of the World. To the world, the people of Michigan, and especially to Detroit, Joe Louis's name has been for decades a symbol of fortitude.

The unmatchable athletic grace and power, the personal integrity and humility have marked the Brown Bomber as one of the truly great men in the world of sports.

Beginning with that summer night in 1937, the legend of the Brown Bomber grew to become an institution. His twenty-five successive title defenses as well as his unselfish contribution of two entire purses to the army and the navy relief funds during World War II added to that legend.

It is particularly fitting that the people of Detroit have conceived what most certainly will be an unforgettable salute to the Champ—Joe Louis—on August 12, 1970.

Joe Louis's skill and might inside the boxing ring were exceeded only by his warmth and humility outside the ring. He brought honor, pride, and inspiration to his race, his city, his state, and his nation.

THEREFORE, I, William G. Milliken, Governor of

the State of Michigan, do hereby proclaim Wednesday, August 12, 1970, as JOE LOUIS DAY in Michigan, in proud and respectful tribute to one of the century's greatest sports figures.

At the hospital in Denver, a decision had to be made. Should Louis be allowed to go to Detroit? Dr. Martin opposed the trip. "He said that it would interfere with Joe's treatment," Martha would say later. "The doctor believed that Joe was beginning to realize that he belonged in the hospital and took it as a good sign. Of course, Joe said something else to me. He said, 'Martha, I don't trust myself to go to Detroit. I might not want to come back here.' He knew the court order was good only in Colorado."

So Detroit celebrated Joe Louis while Joe himself remained in the psychiatric ward. Martha went to Detroit, accompanied by Punchy and Jacqueline. Tickets to the benefit show cost from $5 to $1,000. Cobo Hall resounded to the sounds of some of the finest black entertainers in the country. And music—hard rock, soul, blues, and ballads —was heard. Mahalia Jackson was there, and so was Billy Eckstine, Louis's friend. The audience laughed at jokes told by Redd Foxx, a comedian, and responded warmly to the songs of B. B. King, the blues singer. And when Bill Cosby, the master of ceremonies, introduced Martha, there was an enthusiastic outburst of applause. Then Punchy came to the stage and told the gathering, "Dad's quite pleased by the whole thing here. He's sorry he couldn't make it." An immeasurable shout of approval went up.

When all the receipts were counted, they amounted

to $80,000. The money was deposited in the Commonwealth Bank of Detroit. To prevent dissipation of the fund, a firm "hold" was imposed on it. "You can be sure," a trustee of the fund said, "that none of this money will go for any other cause than to ensure private medical treatment for Joe Louis."

On the way home from Detroit, Punchy was overcome by a euphoric feeling about his father. He reflected on the great throng that had filled Cobo Hall and later told a friend, "When I was in Detroit and I stood up and the people were cheering, just kept right on applauding, it really felt very warm and touching because I know the only reason they were doing it was because I was a male representative of dad. I guess that is how to describe what it means to be a son of Joe Louis."

The next weekend, Punchy made it his business to play golf with his father. They formed a foursome with Billy Eckstine, who was performing at a Denver hotel, and another of Joe's friends, a visitor from Baltimore. Louis and Punchy talked a great deal; and when they were driving home from the course, Punchy said, "Dad, I really got a kick out of playing golf with you today." His father responded, "It makes me happy for you to say that."

When he returned to the hospital on Monday, Louis told Dr. Martin he had enjoyed playing golf with his son. Dr. Martin was pleased until Louis added, "But I saw two or three men from the Mafia out there."

38

A pleasant day in Denver. Louis sat on a bench under an awning to shield him from the sun. The patients of Seven North had just finished a putting contest on the hospital lawn. Louis, the winner, had collected first prize of two dollars, which he stuffed into a pocket in his baggy trousers. They were blue. He wore a tan pullover shirt and brown shoes. He appeared tired, mostly because he was unshaven. The stubble on his cheeks and chin was streaked with gray, in contrast with the blackness of his unkempt moustache. A fellow patient carrying a framed miniature painting approached him. The watercolor, a moderately successful seascape, was thrust at Louis. Its appearance altered Louis's mood.

"Your wife ordered this," the painter said.

"How much?" Joe asked.

"Five dollars."

Louis pushed his hand into his pocket and pulled out the two dollars he had just won. "Ain't enough," he said. "Better wait until she comes to pay you." He spoke to a friend sitting on the bench with him. "That boy's pretty good at that painting stuff. He makes a few dollars selling them to other patients."

As he spoke, he turned and looked behind him apprehensively, his eyes finding the windows of Seven North. "That's where I stay," he said, "where the wire mesh is on the windows." He changed the subject abruptly. "You know, people are real nice. I get a lot of letters from people wishing me luck, telling me to get better. Some of them send money, not much. Some dollars, maybe five dollars. I hope Martha writes them letters thanking them."

Another patient sitting nearby with his wife and a young son pointed at Louis. "See him," he said to his wife. "He knocked out Schmeling, and Hitler walked out of the stadium."

Louis laughed. "That was Jesse Owens in the 1936 Olympic Games," he corrected the other patient without addressing him.

"You remember Hitler walked out of the stadium in Berlin when Jesse won all them events. Hitler didn't like a black man winning all them medals. They got me mixed up with Owens."

"He didn't like you beating Schmeling either," Louis's friend said.

"No, but he wasn't there, and he didn't walk out of no stadium, not that night."

"That was a long time ago."

"Things are different now," Louis said.

"Would you be a black militant if you were the champion now?"

"Maybe. In my time they still had the Ku Klux Klan around and nobody talked loud about the way things were, and they were bad. I guess I'd be different if I was the champion now, the way athletes are talking up."

Again, almost guardedly, he turned and peered over his shoulder in the direction of the windows of Seven North.

"You worried about something, Joe?"

"Ain't worried," he said. "I'm just thinking about them assholes blowing gas in on me." He looked at his fingers, which were tobacco-stained. "You got a cigarette?" he asked a patient standing nearby. When he was given one, he used two matches to light it. He held the cigarette daintily, and when he put it between his lips he did not inhale the smoke. "One thing I want to tell you," Louis said, "I feel better here than I did in a long time. Naturally, I get good rest. And that medicine helps. I got to go take some now." He got up from the bench and walked along a concrete path leading to the hospital. Before he entered, he turned and looked up at the windows of Seven North. The wire-meshed windows gleamed in the strong summer sunshine.

39

Under Colorado law, Louis's commitment to the hospital could be extended for another three-month period if it was deemed medically advisable. By August, Dr. Martin offered the opinion that Louis should remain in the hospital. Although he was pleased with his patient's progress, he believed that Louis's "delusional concerns" had not completely disappeared. But by the next month, Dr. Martin decided that Louis had sufficiently extricated himself from his paranoic darkness to be permitted to travel outside the state. This involved a risk. If Louis decided not to return to Colorado, to remain outside the state's jurisdiction, nothing could be done to bring him back to Denver. Accompanied by Martha, Louis went to Las Vegas on Friday, September 18.

No lapse in reality contact occurred during Louis's weekend stay at Caesars Palace. The first night he was there he did some gambling, and when he finally got to bed, he was pleased with himself. So was Martha. He slept late and awoke on Saturday morning to be greeted by Resnick, who presented him with a new sweater. That afternoon, they played a round of golf. Devoid of tension, Louis appeared happy. By Monday he was back in Denver. The experience had proved so heartening to all concerned it was freely believed that Louis was on his way to the recovery of a meaningful sense of security. The patient was placed on "day status," which meant that he could sleep at home and report back to the hospital each morning for private and group therapy.

This evaluation was further endorsed by Dr. Martin a month later. On October 16, he composed a report on Louis's condition. After describing the course of his patient's paranoia, Dr. Martin wrote, ". . . although his delusional concerns have by no means completely disappeared, it is currently felt that the continuation of his treatment could well be handled on an outpatient basis. The patient can resume employment or activity. . . ." He discharged Louis and prescribed doses of fifty milligrams of Thorazine four times daily and fifty milligrams at bedtime. He also directed Louis to continue to take twenty-five milligrams of Hydrodiuril, the diuretic, each morning.

As an outpatient, Louis saw Dr. Martin at the hospital twice a week. His response to the therapy was indicated in a decrease in his "delusional concerns and an increase in his ability to tolerate minimal amounts of anxiety and affect." For two months Louis adhered to his schedule of appointments with Dr. Martin. In mid-December, Dr. Martin told Louis that there would be a two-week lapse in the course of treatment. He explained that he had to go into a hospital for minor surgery and would be unable to see Louis. About this, he would later write:

"I believe that his fantasies about my surgery plus his not being able to meet with me evoked more discomfort in him than he was able to tolerate; and he again became severely delusional and resistant to the notion of therapy. Following this, he refused to return for his therapy sessions, became much more fearful, and his delusional thoughts generalized. Contact with close friends, relatives, and a private physician revealed that he had regressed to a point of emotional disturbance at least as severe, if not more so, as he had when he was first admitted to my care."

By then, Louis was spending all his time in Las Vegas. He was out of Colorado and never going back.

40

One day in January 1971, Louis sat in the casino at Caesars Palace. He had been playing blackjack with his usual bad luck and had turned to Keeno with the same result. Then, meeting a journalist who had come to talk with him, Louis said, "Let's get out of here." He looked around him, his attention caught by several tourists approaching with paper and pen extended in his direction. "Can we have your autograph?" a diminutive woman wearing puce shorts and blouse asked. "It's for my little grandson back in Oregon." His jowly face had been a picture of unsparing sternness. But now, signing the paper for the little woman, he suddenly seemed generous and carefree. "Say hello to your grandson for me," he said, and there was laughter. He wrote his name several more times and when the tourists went away, he turned in his chair and said, "We can talk here." The opportunity to talk seemed to delight him. But that was an inaccurate impression. Grimly, he was soon recounting his delusions concerning Helen Dayton and the Mafia plot to destroy him with poison gas.

"You got to tell the whole story," he said. "She's in on it. What they tried to do was to get moving pictures of me in bed with her. She had this chauffeur, and he was helping her. They were in with the Mafia; and when I found out, they started trying to kill me. That's why they keep pumping that gas in on me. Martha's in it, too. She made a loan off the Mafia and couldn't pay it back, and they said she had to help them get rid of me. It's all of them together. I tried to get Helen to confess, but I couldn't. I talked to a lot of people. They were all in on it, even some of them that said they're friends. And Martha put me in that hospital. She used Punchy to do it. He didn't know what he was doing.

"Even the way I went to the hospital in New York that time, when I collapsed in the car, that's part of it. I was staying with this friend in his place in New York and the night before I collapsed this woman—white woman—called me on the phone and asked for a hundred and fifty dollars I owed her. It was for a quarter of cocaine. A quarter—that's how they measure it when they sell it to you. So she came up to the apartment, and I paid her the hundred and fifty. She said, 'Joe, here's another quarter for you. This is free. You just take it without paying me.'

I didn't think there was anything wrong with it.

"That night I didn't sleep good, so I took some cocaine. Sniffed it. You know how you do it?" Not waiting for an answer, he pulled a pack of matches from a pocket in his trousers and carefully tore off the lower half of the open cover. He folded the torn section in half so that it formed a sort of funnel and raised it to his right nostril.

"It's called a 'quill.' You put the cocaine in it and sniff it up into your nose. I guess I been around this stuff a long time, with all those show people who took it. I started when I was feeling bad, but I was never strung out on it. It just made me feel relaxed, like that time in New York. Only it made me sick then. That woman gave me bad cocaine. She must be in with the Mafia. I drank a lot of milk to wash my stomach, but it didn't help.

"I went on a television show the next morning, and the hot lights were bad for me. So when we were riding downtown, me and Abe and some others, I got sick in the car, sweating all over. They took me to the hospital, and I told them there about the cocaine. That's how come they pumped my stomach. It saved my life."

Louis sat quietly. He removed the golf cap he was wearing and disclosed his depleted hair. His face, puffy, was suddenly in repose. "I don't touch that stuff no more," he said.

41

Worldwide reaction to Louis's illness had been sober and compassionate. Nothing that had happened to him in the years since his abdication had altered the affection in which he was held. The long shadow cast by his illness was not discernible to those who knew him publicly as a great old former champion. And when he came to Madison Square Garden on March 8, 1971, to see Joe Frazier defend the world heavyweight championship against Muhammad Ali, the huge throng in the arena arose and delivered itself of one long cheer. Nobody else introduced from the ring, not even Frazier or Ali, evoked so responsive a sound, though Louis had not thrown a gloved fist in twenty years. Louis, attired in a dark suit, appeared self-assured, jaunty, even prosperous, in rich contrast to the anguished figure he represented privately. He had long been accustomed to the cheers, and he had always reacted with appropriate dignity, outwardly unmoved, inwardly warmed. And now, in the fifty-seventh year of his time, he somehow retained, against all odds, the same captivating quality. He will never lose it. He is a man of history, transcending time, reaching beyond the limits of the sports world in which he first became famous.

No more certain proof of this comes to mind than the reaction of the "live" audience at the annual awards ceremony of the National Academy of Television Arts and Sciences at the Hollywood Palladium on May 9, 1971. The aristocracy of the electronic world filled the large auditorium for the spring rite, there to pay witness to the achievements of members of their own order. When each of their peers was awarded an "Emmy," they applauded warmly, without anybody rising from his seat to cheer.

Then came Louis, who had been invited to present an "Emmy" to Roone Arledge, president of ABC Sports and creator of ABC's "Wide World of Sports." In keeping with the sartorial demands of the event, Louis wore a dinner jacket. Clean-shaven, his face gleamed under the bright lights aimed at the podium by television technicians. Louis did not speak. He seemed to be fixed by a sense of timing as acute as a nightclub comedian's. In an instant he was washed by echoing and reechoing applause. The entire audience stood and the ovation went on and on. And all the while Louis just stood there, impassive as always, reacting as he had in earlier, happier days, when assorted gladiators had fallen before his fists. And when he finally spoke, his words somehow were unimportant. Only the man, the figure of a good and great man, was remembered, though he had a long way to go along a road still uncharted and mostly dark.